CREATE YOUR OWN
STAGE COSTUMES

Uvania,
Thank you so much
for your hard work
and dedication. It
has been greatly
appreciated. We hope
you'll be able to use
this book ☺

Katie
Cream

Chris
Cam

Janni
Megan Shannon
Watson

Danny
Scott

Cristin
Beavers

CREATE YOUR OWN
STAGE COSTUMES

Jacquie Govier and Gill Davies

A & C Black · London

Heinemann · New Hampshire

First published 1996 by
A & C Black (Publishers) Limited
35 Bedford Row, London WC1R 4JH

ISBN 0-7136-4261-0

Published simultaneously in the USA by
Heinemann,
A division of Reed Elsevier Inc.,
361 Hanover Street,
Portsmouth, NH. 03801-3912

Offices and agents throughout the world

Distributed in Canada by
Reed Books Canada,
75 Clegg Road, Markham,
Ontario L6G 1A1

ISBN 0-435-08675-8

CIP catalogue records for this book are
available from the British Library of Congress.

Create your own Stage Costumes
was conceived, edited and designed by
Playne Books, Trefin, Haverfordwest,
Pembrokeshire SA62 5AU,
United Kingdom

Editor
Gill Davies

Designers and illustrators
Craig John
David Playne

Typeset by Playne Books in ITC Fenice

Printed by Book Print, Spain

Contents

How to use this book

The first section of the book explores the organisation and the planning necessary to run a successful wardrobe department, however small the theatre company and its budget.

Basic sewing techniques, how to alter clothes and fabrics, finishing touches, and converting clothes are then explored in considerable depth in the next two sections, with lots of illustrations to show the various techniques clearly.

Having armed the reader with this essential know-how, the book goes on to evaluate many different types of costume, from accessories to historical costume, from making masks to making a monster.

These sections, in the second half of the book, are full of step-by-step instructions, hints and suggestions, and costume and pattern profiles. Each section begins with a general brief introduction, followed by an exploration of the wide range of possible materials and technique options and, finally, several projects are explained in greater detail.

Please note

Materials and tools are listed for specific projects.

Actions are numbered.

It is assumed that all the seam allowances are approximately 2 cm (3/4 inch) unless otherwise stated.

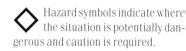 Hazard symbols indicate where the situation is potentially dangerous and caution is required.

Abbreviations

WS = Wrong side

RS = Right Side

While every care has been taken to verify facts and methods described in this book, neither the publisher nor the authors can accept liability for any loss or damage, howsoever caused.

Introduction

Any theatrical performance, whether a musical or pantomime, an historical drama, a thriller or Shakespeare play–indoor, outdoor, in the round, in cabaret or on the street–aims to transport its audience into another world. Theatre creates momentarily a make-believe place where characters appear before us to capture our interest and involve us in their lives and stories. Even for those settings that lie within our immediate experience, we learn much more about the vibrancy of human contact in the ordinary everyday lives of people like ourselves.

Most powerfully, through the medium of drama we delve into experiences beyond our normal ken–we accept speaking animals, understand better the human element in the passage of history, the maelstrom of politics, power struggles in a royal household, the excitement of scientific discovery; the way people live and think in countries and times other than our own. Nightmares can unfold, and the magic of fantasy and fairy tale become tangible.

To achieve all this the actors assume new roles and bring to life human experience–a process initially begun by the playwright but conveyed to the audience through the interpretation of the script by the actors.

One of the greatest assets to both audience and actor in this interpretation is the costume that the actor wears. A good costume can convey immediately all sorts of visual clues to the play as a whole or to scenes within it–its place in time, its location geographically, whether it is a serious or humourous enactment, the mood, the style, the intent. Meanwhile we have an immediate impression of the character–rich or poor, old or young, strong or weak, timid and retiring or extrovert and out to impress, relaxed or highly strung, sloppy or organised.

Clothes express a great deal about people. Anyone who decides on the spur of the moment to offer a lift to a particular hitch-hiker will base that decision on an instant–and often quite distant–aspect of the person waiting on the roadside. Theatre is exactly the same. Notwithstanding that character is explored through voice and intonation, through body language and facial expressions and numerous other acting techniques, the costume makes an enormously powerful visual statement which has an immediate effect and needs to be stated correctly.

This book will help anyone making costumes for a stage play to analyse all the elements and then to decide what is required. What is the overall aim? What are the most pertinent elements of the costume? What are the various ways to do this? Can it be done cheaply enough and in time? What do I need?

But most important of all, when deciding what kind of costume to make, is to understand the play, to understand the character, to use your imagination–and to have fun doing so. There can be no greater reward than seeing a character become alive on the stage and to have had a part in creating this.

Why's and wherefore's: what are costumes for?

General aims of the book

This book is aimed at the amateur theatre, at a company with already limited resources, where time is at a premium and the budget is often inadequate—not to mention the limited abilities of some willing helpers.

In these circumstances, hiring a full set of costumes for a production or making them all from scratch may be inappropriate.

In the following pages it is suggested that the costumier can often adopt a recycling approach towards the theatrical wardrobe, 'ad-libbing' existing garments and/or re-creating them. Moreover, many stage costumes can be made to serve a dual purpose. For example, cuffs and collars can be detachable, and then when these are

removed at a scene change, an apparently new garment is produced! Similarly, a genteel lady's velveteen skirt which made a sedate entrance at

the beginning of the play can become a dramatic cape for a swashbuckling hero later on in the scenario.

This does not mean that the process of making new garments has been abandoned. There are many guidelines on how to make new costumes, using and adapting the basic pattern shapes provided in this book. This has been approached in a fairly simplified way because a set of comprehensive draping, tailoring and stitching techniques can be very intimidating, especially to the beginner.

Generally speaking, most garments discussed in this book have a limited life expectancy, as there is little point in producing extremely elaborate, highly finished, beautifully made garments for, say, just three or four performances. More often than not, quantity is more desirable than quality. However, just occasionally it may be worth taking the plunge and making something for 'keeps'. This can be purely to keep for one's own personal wardrobe or just simply because that particular character costume may be used for other productions.

'or instance, end-of-term school productions frequently have kings, fairies and witches (to mention just a few) cropping up in the most unlikely of plots. An added bonus is that the size span of a particular school-year group hardly varies from one season's production to the next!

Sometimes costumes are coveted by the actors concerned and the purchasing of such items will certainly help to swell the company's bank balance. Apart from these reasons, it is often simply more satisfying, if the time is available, for the costumier to make a thorough job; 'a job worth doing is worth doing well'.

Moreover, certain costumes may be particularly suitable for hiring out to other local drama companies or to individuals as fancy-dress costumes. These will certainly have to take more wear and tear and be more robust than the 'one off' costumes.

Overall, the aim is to analyse exactly what a particular costume needs to convey, to select and concentrate on the most significant elements of an Elizabethan or a 1930 dress, a cat, an angel or a witch costume, and then to convey these essentials to an audience in the simplest and the most effective way—without overspending the budget!

Getting into the character and 'feeling the part'

Why bother with the costumes? Many helpers must echo this thought when submerged beneath a heap of gowns, all requiring hand-sewn hems!

Anyone who has changed from jeans and sneakers into a uniform with heavy boots or worn a sweeping crinoline will instinctively know the answer. Clothes make you 'feel the part'. They affect the way you move, the way you feel about yourself, and even the way others see and treat you.

If you are not sure about this, try, if you dare, dressing up as a punk rocker or maybe a policeman. Or slip into some long eastern robes. See how differently you feel and how the world feels about you.

Consider, too, how some clothes give the impression of authority, whereas unconventional dress suggests an anarchistic approach to life. A neat outfit implies a precise kind of person, whereas a hotchpotch of clothes or colours gives an unworldly air. Think how the cautious pensioner assesses the appearance of a stranger knocking

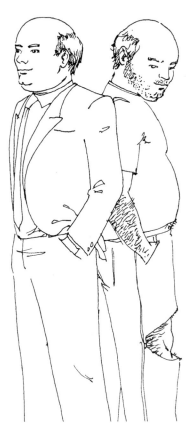

on the door, peering through the curtains and judging the callers largely by the instant impressions that their clothes convey.

Moreover, dress and accessories affect mannerisms. What do you do with your hands? Do you have pockets to swagger with, gloves or a handbag to nervously clutch—or a wrist-watch? The actor who constantly glances at and fiddles with a watch will immediately express anxiety.

How clothes are worn will often supply pointers to build up the picture of a character. The nature and design of clothes affects so much of our daily life without our realizing it.

Thus it is with the characters portrayed in the theatre. It is not enough merely to speak the lines; the actor must feel in character. For this reason, on a purely practical level it is important—particularly with historical roles—that temporary rehearsal costumes should be worn until the actual garments are ready. The actor needs to find out what limitations the garments may impose, apart from using them to help create the feel of the character.

A cloak swung casually over a shoulder could easily topple many of the stage props, or a crinoline might be difficult to squeeze through a doorway—with an awkward exit sometimes producing quite an unsuitable overexposure of underwear! Remember that a man wearing tails must learn how to sit carefully. There are many such practical considerations to come to terms with and, hopefully, the temporary costume will be the catalyst to instigate a character metamorphosis.

Occasionally costume limitations can have a bonus. Such is the case with a

Learning to cope with a crinoline has its hazards!

Victorian woman's outfit because a free-moving 'emancipated' modern actress will be forced to maintain an upright stature when squeezed into a Victorian waspee. Her forthright speech is bound to be reduced to breathless repartee! Also, actors who use swords have to learn how to manage these safely.

Style and stylization in costume design

Often these two words are misinterpreted and so it is prudent to discuss them at this particular stage, especially focusing on the stylization aspect. Needless to say, these comments will be limited purely to aspects concerning fashion. However, in principle most of the components of a theatrical production can be viewed from such a standpoint.

Style refers to general and individual life-styles set within confines of place and time. In relation to fashion, style is a comment on life-style–how costumes were worn, when they were worn, where they were worn, and so on. It reflects an overall feeling of age, yet encompasses the details and characteristics of a specific historical era.

For instance, a king's clothes will convey something quite different from those of a medieval serf–in other words, they signify authority versus subservience.

Style even gives us a clue to the very nature of a character: an ebullient and flamboyant role or a tentative weak temperament can be indicated by visual image alone. However, one can still generalize and refer to a particular style–for instance the 1920s style.

Stylization, however, suggests a theme. It is the selecting of certain aspects of within a 'style' usually so as

to create a visual a visual impact or to simplify a theme- thus one can say that a production was a 1920s stylized piece. In such an instance an audience would be very much aware of the stamp of the designer, who in effect had selected only that which he or she felt was important, rather as an artist selects certain aspects of a scene while a camera lens has to incorporate everything that is there.

For instance, keeping to the 1920s theme, in a stylized musical the men might wear brightly coloured, vividly striped blazers with co-ordinating plain trousers; the women could wear striped cloches with tubular, short dresses to match the men's trousers. The colours would be historically incorrect, but the designer will have selected the essential shape, or silhouette, of the Twenties, thus stylizing the Twenties fashion scene.

On the other hand, this does not have to be part of an historical context. The theatrical costume designer can view the problem from a different slant.

Consider colour for instance. Simple bold colours which are also echoed by the make-up, props and set can have a tremendous visual impact. Black and white clothes in conjunction with strobe lighting is very dramatic. Red, orange and yellow give a tremendous feeling of warmth and heat, whereas blues and greens immediately suggest colder climes, subdued emotions or a sea theme.

Shapes are another angle around which to formulate ideas and can be symbolic where many conventional fashions cannot be, with, for example, simple stark lines reflecting an austere society and flamboyant flowing costumes to symbolize freedom. Pattern and fabric design are singu-

rly more complex to consider in this
eld, and to discuss this in any detail
ou will need to have a particular pro-
uction in mind.

s a general rule, remember that cos-
ume shapes and fabrics are an
xtension of the sets or the backdrops,
nd characters can be made up and
ressed to be a part of this, to emerge
r to blend as required.

Many other themes can be considered.
or instance, in a 'propaganda' play
he players could be dressed as if they
ere wearing newsprint, each bearing
 headline. A mythological character
ould be made up and dressed to look
ke mosaic or a saint like a stained-
lass window.

ometimes (and this is particularly
elevant to school productions) masks
an be used. Each member of the cast
ears a leotard and tights and dons a
nask to give the audience a pointer
owards their identity. Of course many
reek plays were originally per-
ormed in this stylized manner. The
raditional masks each bore a 'styl-
zed' expression to convey particular
motions, and thus were created the
amous comedy and tragedy masks of
he theatre.

ive yourself plenty of time to explore
ll of the possibilities if you are
nvolved with a stylized production: it
is particularly important to share
thoughts and ideas with the director
and the other design members of the
production. The thought processes of
selection, and the application of such
ideas, are often more time-consuming
than a conventional approach to
design but the sucessful blending of
ideas can be very effective, dramatic
and rewarding. However, the particular company's financial standing and
the play's budget must be considered,
as this method often eliminates the
possibilities of improvising with any
existing garments and trims.

Costumes to 'fit the bill' have to be
made from scratch or hired–quite
often at considerable expense. This
will need to be discussed with the rest
of the production team when the budget is considered.

A final thought

Whatever the style of the production
and the scope of the budget, be sure
you make the most of the facilities that
are available–the pool of sewing talent within the group, the ideas of
others and whatever sources of materials you can find. Above all, remember that creating costumes is an
artistic endeavour. Be adventurous,
be imaginative and try to introduce
some extra flair.

Getting organized

The responsibility for dressing the cast can seem quite daunting at the beginning of a production, especially if there is a large cast and a short period of time before 'curtain up'.

Whatever the play or the costume demands, the most important factor is to be organised and in control, to plan well and delegate carefully, making sure that all those helping are aware of the style of the production and the overall purpose of each costume.

Creating a design

So you want to be a designer?

Dressing a play provides a wonderful opportunity for experimentation and exploring cut and fabric.

To dream up design ideas is one thing but to convey them to others is quite another. Anyone who wishes to design successfully will need to be able to communicate his or her ideas clearly with all other parties concerned—such as the director, set-designer, sewing helpers, cast or whoever.

It is very useful to be able to illustrate costume designs, especially if the sewing tasks are to be delegated. It is all too easy for a 'puffed sleeve' or a 'dropped waist' to be interpreted quite differently by someone else.

Figure sketching simplified

If the prospect of drawing figures seems intimidating, then to try and trace them may be far easier. Buy a roll of tracing paper—or better still, use a light box (see opposite page).

An out of date mail-order catalogue or a dress-pattern book will supply suitable figures to trace. Choose those with the most obvious body shape, such as models who are wearing trousers and figure-hugging sweaters, or parading in swimwear; perhaps the more explicit underwear pages may be useful! If all else fails, the cardboard dress-up dolls in a child's book may serve the purpose.

Following the body contours, trace only the outline of the figure, using a dotted or broken line. Then indicate the waistline and the positioning of any seams that may be relevant.

Transfer those outlines that satisfy your requirements on to sketch paper using tracing paper; or by 'scribbling' on the reverse and then redrawing them. Photocopy a good number of these 'prototype' figures so there will be sufficient to allow experimentation with different sorts of design.

Now explore the effects of various necklines, hems, waistlines, and so on. It is surprising, for instance, the difference a new trouser length or sleeve shape can make to the overall appearance of a costume.

It may be worthwhile looking at some books on the history of fashion in order to find inspiration! Also, thumbing through fashion magazines will help to develop an understanding of just how material drapes over the body. When creating historical costumes, do remember that each era presents its own special silhouette and this must always be borne in mind when designing for a play.

Communicate and plan

1 Read the play so you understand these requirements and can talk sensibly to all the others concerned in the production.

2 Obtain a list of the casting so that you can 'study form'.

3 Rough out some ideas to discuss with the producer. Start rummaging and collecting for whatever is needed.

Do not forget to check the existing wardrobe for anything that might be suitable.

4 Talk to the producer and discuss how the costumes can help communicate both the characters and the feel of each scene to the audience.

5 Talk to the designer and to the lighting personnel to check how the costumes can contribute to important colour schemes or to atmospheres being created.

6 Talk to the cast about how *they* see the characters too.

7 Measure the cast. This can be a difficult task to undertake at rehearsals. Actors always seem to be needed on stage the minute the tape measure is wrapped around a bustline or creeping up an inside leg. This is another reason why it is useful to be thoroughly familiar with the play sequence so that you ensure you measure actors well clear of their appearances.

Be considerate. Go into another room if possible. Do not talk loudly and distract those on stage and do not announce to the world any vital statistics that might be embarrassing for their owners.

8 Now go away and think and plan in greater detail

Using a broken line, trace a simple outline of the figure. If required, indicate any important seams.

Transfer the tracing on to the sketch paper. Then add costumes, hat, shoes, and hairstyle–and any relevant details or props.

Experiment with a variety of costume options until you are satisfied you have achieved the desired effect.

Remember to check the combined effects of the designs and colours of the costumes of those characters who appear on the stage simultaneously.

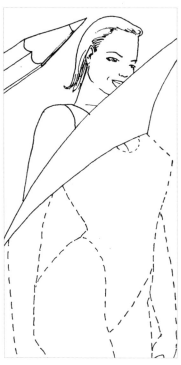

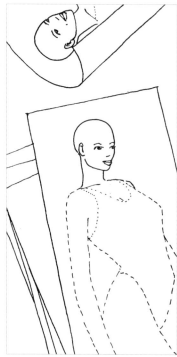

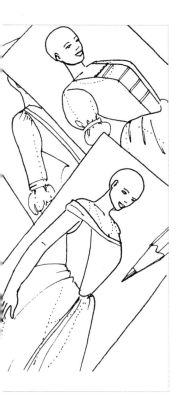

Making your own light box

A light box is very useful. It enables a picture to be illuminated from behind so that it can be copied directly on to the sketch paper. This is considerably easier and less time-consuming than having to trace a picture and then laboriously transfer this copy on to paper.

It is quite simple, when using a light box, to mix or overlap drawings and to see at a glance the effect of this–before actually embarking on the sketch.

You will need

A light source - An angle-poise or adjustable spot lamp

Top
A sheet of glass
Make sure this is not too lightweight. A piece about 12 x 10 inches (304 x 253 cm) will be a workable size but it is best to buy one that is already cut and then fit the other measurements around this

Base
Foam board
This is a board made up of polystyrene foam sandwiched between two layers of card. It is light, sturdy, and easy to cut and can be purchased from most art and craft suppliers

Tools
Craft knife
Metal rule
Cutting board
Scissors

Extras
Cloth-backed adhesive tape or masking tape
Tracing paper (which must be the same size as the glass, so it can be taped on to it to diffuse the light)

It is relatively easy and inexpensive to make a light box, as follows:

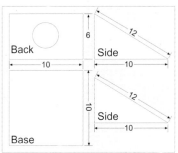

1 Cut the foam board (to suit the size of glass purchased) into the shapes indicated.

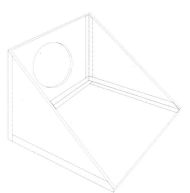

2 Using masking tape or cloth-backed adhesive tape, assemble and tape the foam-board pieces together. Make sure all the junctions are securely joined.

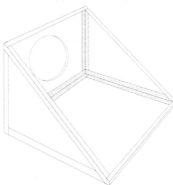

3 Tape the glass into place. A double layer of tape will make the joint

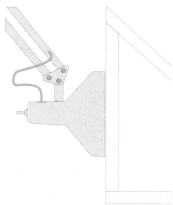

4 Direct the light through the hole a the back of the box.

5 Put tracing paper over the glass t diffuse the light and tape thi securely into place.

6 To use: place the picture which is to be copied on to the illuminated glass 'window'. Cover this with the drawing paper and then trace outline with pen or pencil.

nalysing costume requirements

Name
Address
Telephone and fax
Height
Waist
Chest/bust
Arm length
Inside leg
Hat size
Shoe size
Role
Period
Class
Age
Time of day
Dominant personality traits
Colour/fabric options
Plot requirements
Number of costumes
Any quick changes
Special notes

o be a successful costumier in the mateur dramatic field, first and fore-ost you must be good at lists! Using a hart like the one shown above will elp. (See also page 24 for more details n measuring.)

he initial and most important list is he one which records the phone num-ers and addresses of the helpers. It is lmost impossible to contemplate lothing a medium-to-large company vithout plenty of help. For this reason , t is important that you learn to dele-ate clearly, simply, and precisely and re properly organised (yet more lists).

Once you have read the script, make a st of the characters, noting their ages. Remember, apart from the historical ccuracy of the costume, style also ndicates the character's age and per-onality.) Also make a note of any ostume properties that are mentioned hroughout the script.

Assemble fabric swatches and assort-ed trimmings in acceptable colour combinations as soon as you have decided specific colours and fabrics for particular characters. Staple these sample swatches to your designs.

If the play is set within an historical context you will need to research the period, not only for costumes but for accessories as well. If the play is mod-ern or thematic, discuss colour, design, and shape with the set-designer. (The producer, property, and lighting per-sonnel could also come in at this stage for an open discussion on the general aims of the production.) The form the play should take, its style, mood, impact, and continuity can be assessed by all concerned.

Experimenting with fabrics

It can be very useful to see just how a costume will look if made up in a specif-ic fabric. In order to do this, cut out and remove the costume area from one

sample sketch, so as to create a space where the clothing will be. Now slide a piece of the proposed material under the 'hole' to judge its effect. Experi-ment with a variety of fabric swatches and textures of material and try out dif-ferent colour combinations. Be careful, however, not to cut up your 'master' prototype design!

Starting to create your own costume designs in this way and building up a versatile 'wardrobe' of ideas can be very useful and rewarding.

If you have access to a computer with a colour printer or a colour copier, it is possible to explore an enormous range of colour and pattern effects, provided the budget permits. Colour copies and print-outs are quite expensive but the versatility of experiments is exciting and may inspire all sorts of new ideas.

Making a start

Inspiration may be drawn from many different sources, including books, paintings and photographs. If the production demands it, visit museums to clarify your understanding of how and when period costumes were worn, and what accessories accompanied them.

Make the most of your community. Exploit local talent and businesses. Some fabric centres will give you 'end of the roll' pieces and remnants or allow you to purchase certain fabric ranges at greatly reduced prices. Occasionally stores will loan out outfits for just a mention on the theatre bill.

Let it be known amongst the company and their friends that 'cast-off' clothes are required to form a 'wardrobe pool' for improvised costumes. Give some direction on the type of garments needed: for instance, old curtains, sheets, shirts, skirts, and scarves are all fairly adaptable but much depends on the requisites of the particular production in hand. There will not be great call for 'corsets or stays' in a production of *Journey's End!*

Make a list of the garments offered, specifying colour and size. Don't accept anything unless you have a use for it or you will disappear under a pile of jumble. Suggest diplomatically that surplus offerings can be kept in the owners' attics for forthcoming productions!

You will need to analyse the production's costume requirements very carefully. The amateur costumier is caught up in a delicate balancing act: to hire, or to make. For an elaborate character costume, hiring will often be the less expensive alternative. More often than not, to make such a thing, even with imaginative improvisation, will require many expensive trimmings and possibly the purchase and dying of special fabric; and this will all take up a great deal of time.

The original designs can be stored adequately in an A3 or A4 ring binder.

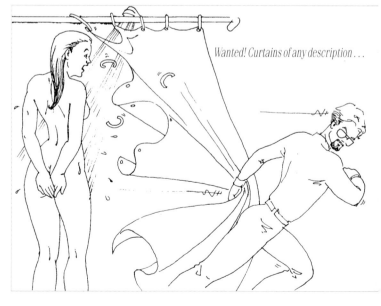

Wanted! Curtains of any description . . .

lear polythene bags held in such a way are extremely useful for filing away designs–along with patterns, fabric and trimming samples, picture references, and even oddments of jewellery. A short length of masking tape (for easy removal) seals the tops of the bags. Colour code the bags (one for each character) with protruding tags, using an index at the front of the binder for easy reference. Remember, do not hand over the original designs to anyone else, only the copies.

Meet your helpers as soon as possible. They will need a précis of the production and a rough outline of the characters involved. Show them the designs. You will find some people will be drawn to particular costumes straight away, wishing to create the whole outfit. Others may prefer to work together as a team, whereas some may feel able to do only small jobs, hand-sewing, or possibly cutting out. It is your responsibility to make the best of your helpers, delegating

where necessary, and finding out where your team's abilities lie.

Of course it is inevitable that there are certain tasks which must go to those who have suitable tools or space for the job concerned (such as a sewing machine with embroidery stitches, washing facilities for dyeing, or even

Do not disturb . . . I'll swap my buttonholes for your hemming.

industrial sewing machines for the heavier jobs).

Do not forget to colour code the helpers' names so that they tally with the colour-coded costume files; this will ensure you know exactly *who* is doing *what*.

Take notes during this preliminary discussion with the helpers: many useful comments are bound to arise and do make sure you are always open to suggestions from the team. A cross-fertilisation of ideas can only improve the costume concepts.

To maintain enthusiasm once the jobs are sorted out, it is a good idea for the costume 'task force' to meet regularly during the allotted time span of the pre-production period. Problems are bound to occur and meeting again will help to clarify these and produce a self-help approach between the 'team'. If the atmosphere is 'fun', the work load will seem less.

A stitch in time

Although it shouldn't happen, occasionally accidents do occur at the last minute. A dress might tear, a seam part, or a button come off. A box of sewing items will always have to be kept somewhere near the wings. If there is time, a needle and cotton can be employed; otherwise staple hidden seams, cellophane tape hems or use a dab of fast-drying adhesive to stick Velcro to fabric.

If an iron can be used off stage, adhesive hemming tape or mending tape can be particularly useful, especially when a snap fastener needs to be replaced. A set of felt pens or crayons

can be employed as temporary cover up for this 'botched up' repair work. And when only a few seconds are available, the inevitable safety-pin repair has saved many an actor from appearing unsuitably torn or undressed!

The costume mistress or master should organise backstage help for such emergencies and with any quick changes. It is not necessary to put in a personal appearance each night. This task can be delegated to a team of people but someone well informed of the requirements must be there each night. The cast will have a far greater sense of security if a reliable unruffled person is immediately available to cope with any problems.

Storage

A major headache for the wardrobe mistress or master is storage, not only for the costumes themselves, but also for their respective accessories. Keeping the right things together is often a problem. A logical system of storing and a simple system of accessibility has to be evolved. Of course this book can only generalise, as specific solutions must be tailor-made to suit the individual company's space allocation, which is, quite simply, never enough!

The wardrobe master or mistress has to adopt a pigeon-hole mentality, if only to keep sane–then perhaps the cast's tempers will remain cool and the production will be staged on time! There has to be a place for everything and everything has to have its place. At this point it must be added that actors and actresses should not take their costumes home during the production period, no matter how tempting this might be. It only takes one forgetful actor to 'throw a spanner in the works' or to put it more appropriately 'draw the curtains on the production'!

To start with, lists have to be made once again. Make a list of the characters, colour-coded to correspond with the costumier's master set of designs in the ring folder. Pin this list up for all to see, on a wall or possibly a screen, replicating this list as necessary if more than one room is used for wardrobe storage.

The colour-coding system should be extended to the hangers, plastic bags, or whatever is used for storage.

If you run out of single colours, create colour combinations or use shapes (such as stars, circles and so on) for easy identification. Tapes, ribbons, or labels will do this. Hopefully this method will create an 'at a glance' means of identification. Also these hangers, bags, or boxes should be

Shoe rack doubles as a whatnot for costume accessories.

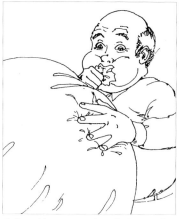

Inflated bag to stop hats being spoilt.

labelled with a tag, on which is written a description of the items within. (This information should also be included on the costumier's master set of designs in the ring binder.)

Such detailed planning may all seem rather laborious but special care taken with the organisation of the wardrobe will hopefully avoid any last-minute panics, when a lost item may well lead to the actor missing a cue on stage.

Refuse sack makes a suitable dust cover for a dress.

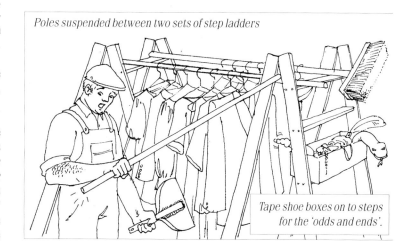

Poles suspended between two sets of step ladders

Tape shoe boxes on to steps for the 'odds and ends'.

Basic tools and techniques

A basic kit: tools for the job

Any dressmaker sufficiently committed to offer his or her services to an amateur theatre company will already have a basic sewing kit but for running a theatre wardrobe several other items will be needed. It is useful to keep a checklist and so ensure that stocks are always adequate for requirements and, as and when required, costed into the production budgets. You will need to find somewhere comfortable to work-ideally a designated area that can be left undisturbed in between sessions and also somewhere where messy tasks such as gluing and dyeing can be undertaken. A source of running water is useful, and good light is essential. Storage will be needed for all the items immediately required as well as those other 'might be useful one day' odds and ends. Preferably keep boxes and jars on easily accessible shelves or in single layers in cupboards or drawers and ensure everything is clearly labelled so it is easy to find.

Wardrobe essentials

Cutting table
If using the dining room table rather than a proprietary worktop, be careful to put a heavy blanket or equivalent over the surface-both to protect table from scratches and to prevent material slithering.

Dress stand

Hanging rail

Iron and ironing board
A sleeve board is a useful extra

Lights
Good source of light

Notebook and files
For measurements of cast and notes on play requirements

Sewing machine
A good reliable user-friendly machine-with zig-zag stitching

Storage containers

Water
Running water and sink

Zink bath or bucket for dying

Haberdashery

Beads

Belts and buckles

Bindings

Braid

Buckram

Buttons

Chalk and soft pencils for marking up fabric

Elastic in various widths

Embroidery threads

Hooks and eyes

Needles
Heavy, lightweight, embroidery-and sewing machine spares

Pins and pin cushions

Press studs

Ribbons

Safety pins

Sheering elastic

Tapes

Threads
A good variety of colours-cotton and polyester plus embroidery threads

Zippers

Materials

Clothes-from secondhand sources

Curtains-velvet and net are useful

Fabric

Metallic foil

Newspaper, brown paper, tissue or tracing paper for making patterns

Sheets

String and cord

Vilene or other stiffening

Wire-milliner's, fuse wire, garden and galvanised wire

Wool

Tools

Cloths and sponges

Eyelet punch and eyelets

Hat block

Kettle

Measuring tape

Paint brushes

Pinking shears

Pliers

Riveting tool and rivets

Scissors

Stanley blades and knives

Stapling machine and staples

Thimble

Yardstick

Other consumables

Adhesives-a variety for different uses. Copydex is good for fabric

Colour and metallic sprays

Fabric and leather dyes and paints

Scotch tape and masking tape

Patterns and cutting out

Any sewing enthusiast will already have a stock of commercial patterns to use but of course when the stage production to be dressed involves large numbers of people and exotic or historic costume, the range of such patterns is likely to be inadequate. Not only is the choice of 'fancy-dress' patterns limited, but also many of the

productions will involve an enormous range of sizes and shapes and it is not feasible to stock the right-sized pattern for every person in every production.

A few basic patterns that have been become 'old friends' over the years always come in handy, however, and familiarity with their particular idio-

syncrasies will enable the dressmaker to adapt them more readily than a brand new pattern.

If a chorus or group are all to be dressed in a matching style then it ma help to begin with one or two sizes of a good basic pattern and then copy and adapt these as necessary. Some pape

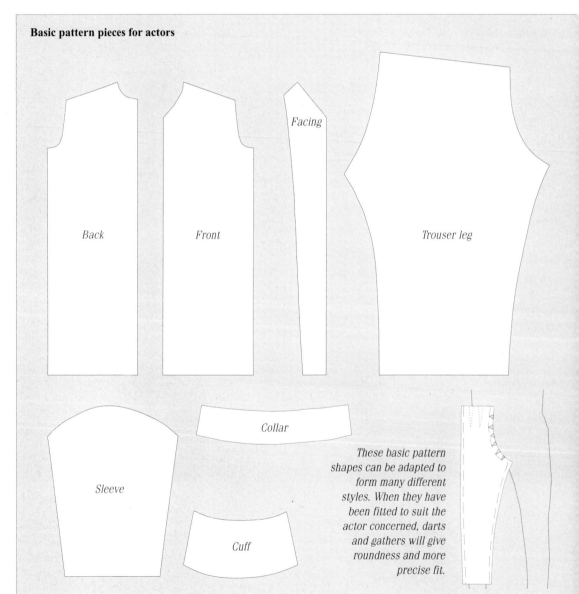

Basic pattern pieces for actors

Back

Front

Facing

Trouser leg

Sleeve

Collar

Cuff

These basic pattern shapes can be adapted to form many different styles. When they have been fitted to suit the actor concerned, darts and gathers will give roundness and more precise fit.

atterns offer a range of sizes on one pattern but the criss-crossing of these variations can be highly complex and confusing and, in practice, they will really work only to fit one size.

Wedding dress patterns encompass a wide range of styles and may be particularly useful for historic costumes.

Commercial dressmaking patterns are expensive so it is probably most useful to invest in a specialist book of patterns for the theatre. There are one or two excellent ones available. Although they may not offer the finesse and fine tuning of purpose-designed patterns, these book patterns have the advantage of being generally less fussy than

conventional ones and therefore more conducive to fast production needs.

Your own pattern drafts and adaptations can be made on newspaper, tissue paper, strong brown paper or tracing paper. They can then be tested against the actors' individual shapes and adjusted to fit.

Basic pattern pieces for actresses

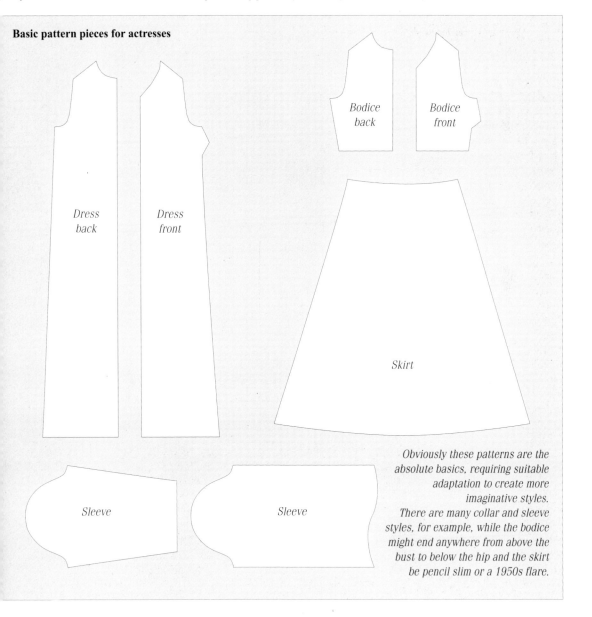

Bodice back

Bodice front

Dress back

Dress front

Skirt

Sleeve

Sleeve

Obviously these patterns are the absolute basics, requiring suitable adaptation to create more imaginative styles. There are many collar and sleeve styles, for example, while the bodice might end anywhere from above the bust to below the hip and the skirt be pencil slim or a 1950s flare.

Measuring up to adapt patterns and garments

One of the easiest ways to begin is to cut up old garments and use these as templates for new garments, always allowing extra seam width. If the actors concerned can be persuaded to part with an old jacket, trousers or dress that fits well, this may help, even if used only as a measure when the actor is unavailable. Make sure such garments are clearly labelled.

To ensure garments fit take the following measurements and keep them on record for future use then you will not have to interrupt the actor to repeat the process in successive productions–except to establish if weight has been lost or gained. Be warned, however, that vanity, panic and no time to eat may spur on weight loss prior to a production and the first fitting may not be the same as the final one!

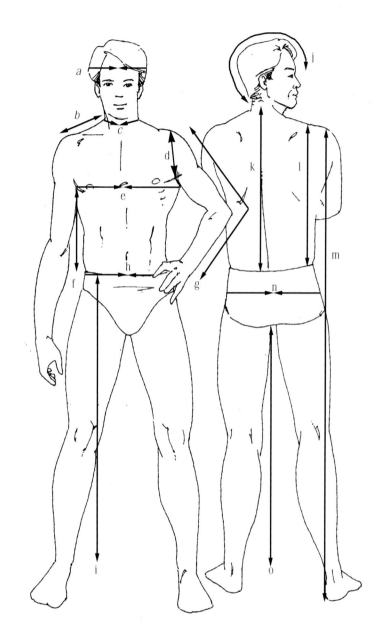

You will need

Tape measure–with inches and centimeters

Pen and indexed note book

Relevant play notes–e.g. if a character needs to be padded out

Paper for drawing round feet

Waterproof pen and name/role tapes to write on, ready for attaching to garments later

Remember: Darts help create the shape needed to accommodate curves, and altering or adding these will adapt a pattern to fit a variety of bustlines and waistlines, as appropriate. Always make generous seam allowances and good hems so that garments can be let out or down for future use.

a	Circumference of head
b	Neck to shoulder
c	Neck (collar size)
d	Armholes
e	Chest/bust
f	Underarm to waist
g	Outer arm–shoulder to wrist (with arm bent)
h	Waist
i	Waist to ankle
j	Forehead to nape
k	Backnape to waist
l	Centre of shoulder to waist
m	Shoulder to ground
n	Hip circumference
o	Inside leg

Hints on cutting fabric

Always work in good light and calm sur-roundings, with lots of room to lay out material and pattern pieces–either on a table or clean floor.

Stop, check and think again to ensure everything is fine before cutting out.

Make sure directions are followed pre-cisely, especially regarding wrong and right sides and the grain of the fabric.

Use sharp scissors–or pinking shears which may help save a lot of tedious 'finishing' of seams and edges.

Do not skimp on pins. It is much easier to cut well if the pattern is attached firmly all round.

Cutting and joining a bias strip

Patterns often require a bias strip. Cutting across the bias of the material can seem wasteful, as taking out a diagonal piece uses much more fabric than cutting a strip from the edge–but do as you are told! The bias strip will have stretch and elasticity which makes it far more pliable and less like-ly to pucker on curved and circular pieces–such as neck and arm bands, waistbands, cuffs and collars–and when making rouleau for frogging and braiding. Always save unwanted cut-off sections and use these.

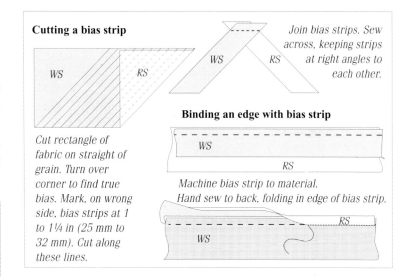

Cutting a bias strip

WS   RS

Cut rectangle of fabric on straight of grain. Turn over corner to find true bias. Mark, on wrong side, bias strips at 1 to 1¼ in (25 mm to 32 mm). Cut along these lines.

Join bias strips. Sew across, keeping strips at right angles to each other.

WS   RS

Binding an edge with bias strip

WS

RS

Machine bias strip to material. Hand sew to back, folding in edge of bias strip.

RS

WS

Body dart sizes

Bust		Bust dart depth
30½ins/775mm	=	½ins/13mm
32½ins/826mm	=	¾ins/19mm
34½ins/876mm	=	1ins/25mm
36½ins/927mm	=	1½ins/38mm
38½ins/978mm	=	1¾ins/44mm
40½ins/775mm	=	2ins/50mm
42½ins 1029	=	2½ins/60mm

Difference between bust and waist		Waist dart width
4ins/102mm	=	½ins/13mm
6ins/152mm	=	¾ins/19mm
8ins/203mm	=	1ins/25mm
10ins/254mm	=	1¼ins/40mm
12ins/305mm	=	1½ins/38mm
14ins/356mm	=	1¾ins/44mm

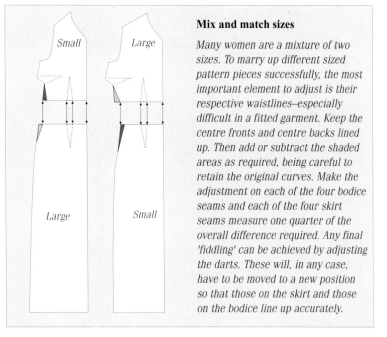

Small   *Large*

Large   *Small*

Mix and match sizes

Many women are a mixture of two sizes. To marry up different sized pattern pieces successfully, the most important element to adjust is their respective waistlines–especially difficult in a fitted garment. Keep the centre fronts and centre backs lined up. Then add or subtract the shaded areas as required, being careful to retain the original curves. Make the adjustment on each of the four bodice seams and each of the four skirt seams measure one quarter of the overall difference required. Any final 'fiddling' can be achieved by adjusting the darts. These will, in any case, have to be moved to a new position so that those on the skirt and those on the bodice line up accurately.

Fabrics

Choosing and finding materials

A good many of the fabrics in the wardrobe may find you, rather than your finding them–especially as existing garments will probably have been inherited or donated but it is good to snap up fabric bargains when they arise and to collect clothes that are not necessarily useful in their present shape but which offer good possibilities for cutting up and using later.

When there is sufficient time to plan well ahead, choosing the right fabrics for the stage can be exciting, and, whatever the budget, offers a great opportunity to experiment. In fact a tight budget is often the inspiration behind the most imaginative ideas.

Colour is very important. Stage colour needs a bold approach and it is fun to create related colour schemes, especially for pantomimes, musicals and revues. Look at colour around you, in the natural world–in flowers and trees, animals, in land, sky and sea scapes, in architecture, in home-decorating schemes, in different geographical locations and the art of historical periods. Think about whatever is appropriate to the play or production style, experiment with paint or crayon or coloured tissue papers to see how your projected colour scheme works .

Acetate
Looks like silk but wrinkles! Good strong colours available and dyes well. Best hand washed or dry cleaned.

Acrylic
Soft, light and fluffy; resists wrinkles and washes well.

Brocade
Rich-looking and excellent for Cinderella ball gowns and 'dressy' occasions for men and women. Expensive new but second-hand evening dresses provide a useful source–good for Regency waistcoats, collars and cuffs. Pad your ironing board well so that designs are not flattened and always test the heat level on a scrap first.

Calico
Plain weave smooth cotton fabric good for patch-work.

Canvas
Good strong material, will take a lot of rough handling! Good for coats, breeches, heavier skirts, uniforms. Also for making belts, and armour, if stiffened with PVA adhesive. Duck, sail-cloth or light weight canvas are good as interlinings for stiffening historical period bodices.

Cheesecloth
Soft and good for gathering and draping, useful as an alternative to muslin if this is not available.

Chiffon
Soft flimsy and light weight. Silk chiffon drapes beautifully but is expensive. Nylon and polyester versions are cheaper but less 'fluid': soaking in a strong solution of fabric softener will help temporarily.

Chintz
Good for Regency and Victorian costumes and finishing touches like collars and purses. Old curtains, cushion and upholstery covers make good sources. Ask in shops for last season's sample upholstery squares.

Corduroy and needlecord
Stiff but good rich pile (cheaper than velvet) and easy to handle; excellent for trousers, jackets, Victorian skirts and riding habits.

Cotton
Crisp and fresh, very adaptable for all sorts of costumes; seams press down well and may hold their own without tacking. It gathers nicely and is the best fabric for 'country' style dresses aprons and pinafores, mob caps and underwear. Sheets are a good cheap source, as well as old dresses and shirts, night-dresses, tablecloths and curtains. Cotton takes dyes well but some types shrink.

Cotton and synthetic mixes
These crease less than plain cotton, and do not fray so easily. They are generally softer, less crisp and have more stretch–very adaptable.

Crepe
Fabric with an interesting crinkled surface. Wool and rayon crepes are especially effective.

Crêpe de Chine
Silk, rayon and nylon versions of this soft crinkled fabric. Good for 1920s and evening wear.

Denim and drill
Strong and adaptable, good for heavyweight skirts, uniforms and tropical wear. Both are strong enough to serve as a base on which to build up to create other layers–for example, a 'jewellery-encrusted' bodice. Old jeans abound and may serve for cowboy costumes, but also provide good source of denim for smaller items, like caps and shoes.

Felt
Can be cut without fraying; may shrink so best to shrink before use but very useful for small decorative features, jewellery, bags, hats, shoes and so on. Industrial or orthopaedic felt can be moulded and stiffened and used as imitation leather or metal (see page 43).

Flannel and flannelette
Wool flannel drapes well and is traditional for men's casual trousers. Thinner cotton flannelette is ideal for night wear.

Fur fabric
Ideal for animal costumes, hats, lining hoods, fur coats and so on. Keep a look

ut for genuine old fur coats, too, which often turn up at jumble sales and attic turn-outs.

Jersey
Lovely soft fabric, but may crease, quite expensive–excellent for Roman and Greek costumes.

Gabardine
Twill weave with a hard surface, this can be a light or heavy fabric–good for uniforms, rainwear and meeting any hard-wearing needs.

Lace
Essential for the historical touch, collars, cuffs, ladies' blouses, ruffs and ruffles, inserts and overskirts.

Leather and suede
Expensive when new but lasts well so old leather or suede is always worth buying when available. Invaluable for accessories and for waistcoats, jerkins and breeches.

Linen
Looks good and drapes well and is strong so good for Greek togas and tunics; some types can crease like hell! Shrinks so either pre-shrink or dry clean. Does not accept dyes well.

Metallic
Effective glittering fabrics which can generally be washed or dry cleaned. Iron at a cool setting.

Muslin
Soft and clinging–good for Napoleonic or Jane Austen styles–less expensive than cheesecloth, especially as sold for household use rather than clothing. Can also be soaked in PVA glue and then moulded into shapes such as ears or fairy wings.

Net
Essential for ballerina tutus, wedding veils and wings but also useful as an alternative to lace if gathered and ruffled and can also serve as a backing for jewellery and so on.

Organdy
Fine, translucent and with a special crisp finish. Today's synthetic versions are wrinkle resistant.

Polyester
Many many kinds with different attributes so very versatile, with all the advantages and easy-washing qualities of synthetic fabrics.

PVC and vinyl
May work as an alternative for leather although it is less hard-wearing and generally shinier; good in its own right for sowesters, bags, mermaid tails, shoes and aprons.

Rayon
Soft and comfortable; drapes and dyes well but can wrinkle or stretch if it is not specially finished and so it is best dry-cleaned.

Sacking
Cheap and rough texture but ideal for any rustic characters. Can be softened and dyed to serve a wider variety of purposes.

Satin and taffeta
Looks lovely in the lights and taffeta has a distinctive rustling noise but both fabrics are expensive when new and can crease–old evening dresses make a good source. Use polyester or silk thread to avoid puckering problems.

Silk
Lovely, luxurious shiny soft fabric –expensive but, once again, jumble sales and 'good as new' shops may turn up trumps. Dyes well and is wrinkle resistant once pressed. Very fine so gathers well and excellent for circular skirts, puff sleeves, overlay skirts, frills, ruffles and so on.

Toweling
Useful for many basic rustic garments. Be careful if you use strech towelling or terry that you use a stretch stitch on your machine or a zig-zag.

Triacetate
Used for garments which need to retain pleats and for sports wear. Resists wrinkles and dyes well.

Tweed
Ideal for any weekend-in-the-country clothes, caps, Sherlock Holmes and the like. Many cheaper look-alike tweeds are available.

Velvet, velveteen and velour
Rich and gorgeous under the lights. Curtains provide a good source.

Viyella
Soft and flowing, ideal for Victorian and children's dresses.

Wool fabrics
Expensive but second-hand sources can be good. Good elasticity; dyes and tailors well. Can prove very warm under the stage lights.

Other sources

Haberdashery remnants.

Upholstery fabrics.

Curtaining, furniture fabrics, chair backs and throw-overs.

Household items:
Towels, tablecloths, sheets, blankets and bedspreads.

Net curtains:
Great for making harem trousers, veils of all kinds, Georgian overskirts (as for Bo-Peep) and Princess dresses; while the scalloped lacy edges can be used around the edges of skirts, sleeves and so on.

Lining material:
This comes in fabulous shades and is inexpensive. It has a lovely sheen but runs like crazy so be sure to seal edges well and to make the fitting generous–it will not endure any rough handling or straining at the seams.

Sewing stitches

Hand sewing

Back stitch

The strongest hand stitch: Bring the needle through to the front of the material and loop each stitch back to where the last stitch ended.

Basting or tacking stitch

This is simply a temporary running stitch with very large stitches that can easily be undone afterwards.

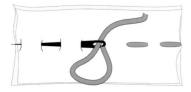

Blanket stitch

Work from left to right, making the first stitch at the edge and succeeding ones about ¼ inch above and over, keeping thread below needle as shown.

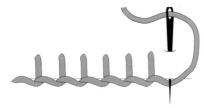

Blind stitch

Used for hemming two pieces together when the stitching needs to be 'invisible' on both sides. Roll the folded edge of the hem back about ¼ inch, then stitch diagonally, catching just a single thread from both hem and garment.

Catch stitch (cross or herringbone)

Good stitch when some flexibility is required. Keep the stitches relatively loose, work from left to right, starting with a small horizontal stitch in the upper piece and then making another stitch in the lower piece of fabric, diagonally across from the first stitch.

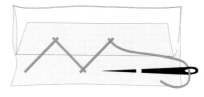

Darning stitch

Place fabric pieces edge to edge. Sew tiny stitches on the outside, just in from the edges, with longer diagonal stitches linking the insides of the two pieces.

Invisible or prick stitch

This variation of the back stich creates a scarcely visible line of stitching. Take needle back just a few fabric threads and keep the surface stitch minute.

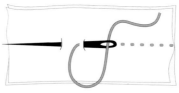

Grafting stitch

This is the same as the oversewing stitch, except that the pieces of fabric are placed edge to edge rather than the two surfaces being held together

Oversewing or overcast stitch

This is useful for making very strong joins or to prevent raw edges ravelling Hold fabric edges together and draw the thread in a spiralling loop over the two edges, keeping the stitches quite close together.

Running stitch

This is the simplest stitch with small evenly spaced stitches on both sides of the fabric.

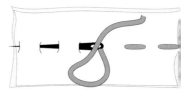

Slip stitch or hemming stitch

Commonly used for hemming. With the turned-up hem facing you, stitch through the top of the turned-up fold Then catch just a single thread from the inside of the garment so that the stitch will be barely visible from the outside.

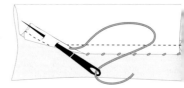

Stab stitch

Stab the needle through from the inside to the outside of the fabric, making longer stitches on the inside and tiny scarcely visible stitches on the outside

Machine stitching

The basic machine stitch is a strong straight stitch locked like a chain stitch by the thread from the bobbin. The smaller the stitch the stronger the join. Longer stitches should be used for decorative purposes, basting or in double rows for gathering. The zig-zag stitch is very useful for finished edges and for decorative purposes. Used densely, it is good for appliqué work. Most sewing machine manuals include detailed instructions on the various stitches that are available and it is good to practise these on spare pieces of fabric to discover the advantages of each and whether there are any particular problems–as every machine has its own 'quirks'. Always ensure threads used for the top stitching and the bobbin are appropriate to the fabric and that the tension is suitably adjusted.

Embroidery stitches

Embroidery stitches add a lovely finishing touch but very fine detail will not necessarily be obvious on stage costumes. Be courageous! Use big bold stitches and rich colours.

Blanket stitch

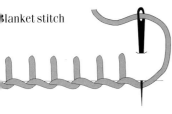

Buttonhole

Chain stitches

Secure thread to garment and then insert needle to the right of this, leaving a loop of thread. Bring needle through again below, catching bottom of first loop and make a new loop. Continue making loops, to create a chain pattern.

Open chain stitch

A chain stitch worked between two imaginary parallel lines

Lazy daisy stitch

is a variation of chain stitch

Feather stitch

Fishbone stitch

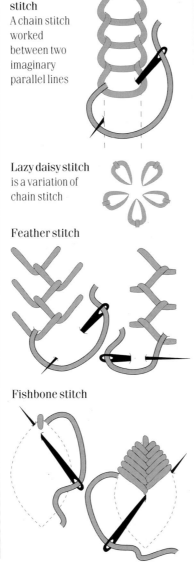

French knots

Herringbone stitch

Overcast stitch

Satin stitch

Stem stitch

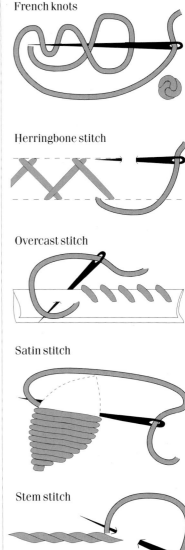

Seams

Seams are basically the joins, the way the different sections of fabric are linked together–and the decision over which seam to use will depend on requirements of time available, the shape of the seam, durability and the finished appearance.

Factors to consider when choosing a seam

Speed

The durability and strength of the seam

The shape of the seam–especially whether or not it is curved and needs ease

The neatness of the finish

Decorative purposes

Stay stitching

To prevent seams stretching, especially on curves, stay stitch along the seam lines first. Always do this *with* the line of the grain. To find the direction of the grain, run your finger along the edge of the cut fabric. The threads *with* the grain will lie smoothly whereas those *against* the grain will begin to come loose and the edge will fray.

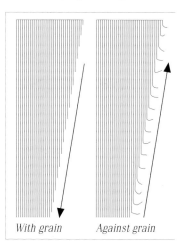

With grain   *Against grain*

Angle seams

Angle seams can be used for figure emphasis or as a design feature.

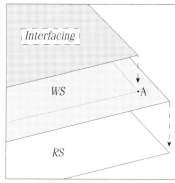

1 Place right sides together, with the corner of the interfacing at A to provide reinforcement.

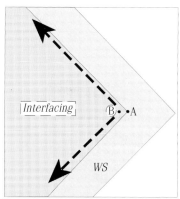

2 Machine away from B in both directions. Keep close to the edge of interfacing. Repeat for extra strength.

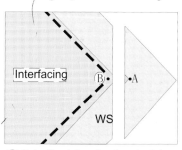

3 Cut off a triangle of material as shown, to avoid bulk at junction.

Corded seams (214 V)

These give a decorative raised emphasis to the seam–useful for a tailored look and uniforms.

1 Cut a length of cord. Make sure it is long enough.

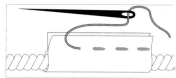

2 Tack, encasing the cording inside bias strip.

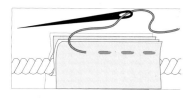

3 Tack encased cording into position; it should be sandwiched between the right sides of fabric.

4 Machine stitch, through all thicknesses, using a zipper or piping foot. Remove tacking.

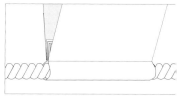

5 Finished piped seam. Trim off any excess cording.

Curved and scalloped seams

To provide ease and 'give' always clip curves and trim the seams as close as possible so that there is no excess fabric and the seam can take up the curves without any 'pulling'.

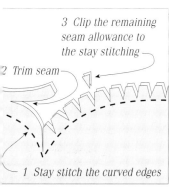

3 Clip the remaining seam allowance to the stay stitching

2 Trim seam

1 Stay stitch the curved edges

French seam

Provides a very neat finish and contains raw edges–good when the inside of the garment will be seen (as on a cloak) and for fabrics which ravel .

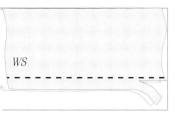

WS

1 Pin wrong sides together and stitch seam. Trim seam close to stitching. Now with right sides together. press along the stitched seam.

RS   WS

2 With the right sides together, stitch along the seam line to enclose the raw edges.

Machine fell seam

Either side can be the right side. this is particularly suitable for shirts and casual clothes.

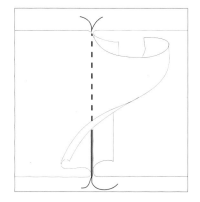

Piped seam

These fulfil a similar function to corded seams, except that the piping is made of fabric, and is not so stiff as cord encased in fabric.

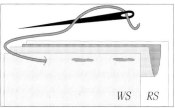

WS   RS

1 Use a folded strip, cut on the bias. Keep all the raw edges together. Baste into position.

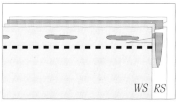

WS   RS

2 Machine stitch through all the layers, keeping inside line of tacking. Trim all of the edges close to stitching.

3 Press, keeping the iron on the right side, alongside the piping.

Slot seam

This is merely a decorative seam which exposes a contrasting fabric; it can be very useful when there is a shortage of material!

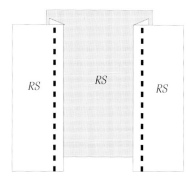

RS   RS   RS

Welt seam

This is a slightly raised seam which is generally intended for decorative purposes. It can be done by hand, using a heavier thread or possibly using a contrasting colour. A stab stitch or a saddle stitch can be used for this.

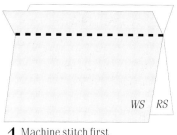

WS   RS

1 Machine stitch first.

RS

RS

2 Press to one side. Trim lower seam allowance to 1/4 inch (6 mm). Stitch through upper seam and garment to enclose cut lower seam allowance.

Hems

The way the final garment fits and hangs will depend upon the way the hem is done. Sometimes it is tempting to rush this in eagerness to complete the garment but a well-executed hem makes all the difference to the final appearance. Sometimes hemming can be delegated to helpers or completed by the actor or actress concerned but always ensure it is given the attention it deserves.

Preparing

Make sure the garment has had time to 'drop' especially if is in heavy fabric or has a full circular skirt.

Measure the fit and mark the hemline clearly. Check which shoes are being worn and the height of heels. Hopefully the actor can wear them for the fitting but this is not always possible.

Pin up hem and then check the final appearance, making any necessary adjustments.

Taking up a hem

To machine, to hand sew, or to glue, that is the question! Much depends on the time available and on the fabric being used. Heavy fabrics and those that fray may need special treatment.

Finished edges

Most hems require a finished edge before the final hem is made. This edge can be sealed with a small turn up (about ½ inch or 1.5 cms).

Alternatively, the edge can be sealed by a zig-zag stitch

. . . or glued

. . . or by sewing on fine tape or bias binding

. . . or cut with pinking shears.

An iron-on adhesive tape can both seal the edge and press the hem into place very quickly.

Copydex and other fabric glues can save a good amount of time and seal edges well when speed is required. Check the effect on the fabric first and apply very thinly. The disadvantage of glues and iron-on tape, however, is that the hem cannot readily be changed again for a taller actor.

A good compromise is to do the first turn-up with glue and treat the final hem conventionally.

Time can also be saved by making the first turn-up secure with pins (played lengthways over turn-up so that they protrude well and can readily be removed later) and then pressing really well so that the turn-up stays in place without tacking.

Generally, the turn-up is most simply achieved by sewing on the machine with a largish stitch.

Assorted hems

At a distance, on stage, generally a machined hem will not show and this can be the simplest and quickest way for lighter fabrics and for very straight hems where there is not too much fullness to contain.

If the skirt is full, it is better to use hand sewing so that you can control and ease the fullness in as you progress. Alternatively, gather in the extra fullness first with gathering stitches before machining.

A variety of hem styles are explained here but bear in mind that too fine close stitching–too good a job in fact–may impede alterations needed for future productions.

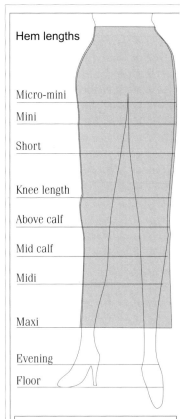

Hem lengths

Micro-mini
Mini
Short
Knee length
Above calf
Mid calf
Midi
Maxi
Evening
Floor

In theory, the hem should always be parallel to the floor but do go along with any optical illusions that might occur with pleats, plaids, or circular and bias cut skirts, accomodating these as best you can–for, ultimately, it is the visual effect that matters.

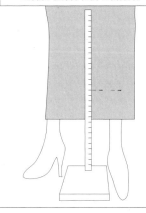

⬝ias tape hem

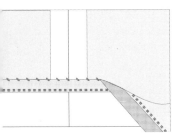

Curved hems gathering in fullness

For circular or curved hems, it is often necessary to make darts or cut V's out of the hem to disperse the fullness.

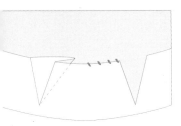

Catch stitch hem

This is especially good for heavier fabrics which can then be pressed without leaving an indentation. An iron can slide under the edges to prevent a ridge showing on the right side.

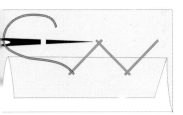

Hems with interfacing

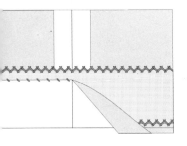

Herringbone stitch

Instead of hemming stitch, herringbone stitch can be used, although this takes considerably longer. If material is thick, bias binding can be used. Stretch lace is also very useful when binding a curved hem.

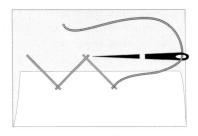

Narrow hem–machine stitched

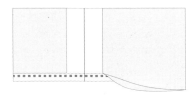

Narrow hand-rolled hem

Narrow hand-finished hem

Pinked hem

Quick effective finish–stops ravelling.

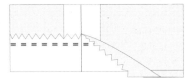

Shrinking a hem

Press a wet cloth or steam iron over a gathered hem to shrink away fullness in a woollen hem. (Remember to fold the hem away from the rest of the garment to avoid overall shrinkage.)

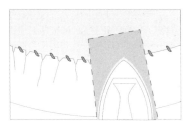

Gathered hems

Gathers can help disperse the fullness.

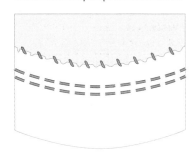

Shell-edged hem

Zig-zag finish–wide and narrow

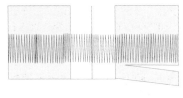

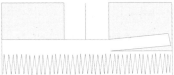

Ruffles, tucks and pleats

Ruffling

Fullness can be softly gathered into a waist, neck or arm band by making long running stitches in at least two parallel rows and then gathering evenly to fit.

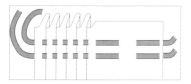

Rouched fabric

Narrow curtain tape is a simple strong way to gather fabric. It is particularly useful as the gathers can be varied according to the required design or size of a garment. Adjustment is simply a matter of tightening or releasing the gathered cords. Vertical rouching is most decorative and suitable for all ball gowns, overskirts and sleeves. The advantage of such decorative rouching on garments is that, once the gathering is released, the garment will appear entirely different and could possibly be used for another character's costume (see page 38).

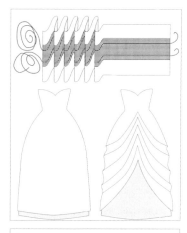

Do not be tempted to cut off the long lengths of cord once the fabric is gathered. Tie the cord into a bow and secure out of sight with a safety pin.

Tucks and pleats

Sometimes it is appropriate, however, to make more formal pleats or tucks.

A tuck is a narrow fold of fabric that may be stitched along part or all of its length. A pleat is a fold of fabric that creates extra but controlled fullness. Both pleats and tucks are best used with fabrics that drape well and are resilient—such as wool, wool blends, silk and synthetics.

Baste tucks and pleats and then press and steam on both sides to set them. Placing strips of brown paper under the pleat before you press it will prevent any nasty ridges or lines appearing on the fabric. Decorative tucks can be stitched on the right side of the fabric with toning thread.

Blind tucks

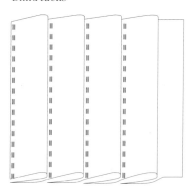

Spaced tucks

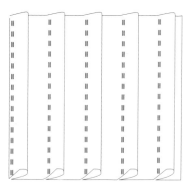

Pin tucks

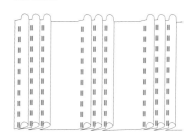

Knife pleats

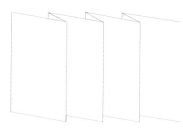

Box pleats

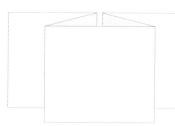

Inverted pleats

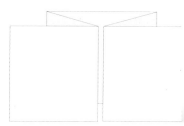

Accordian pleats

Darts, shirring and smocking

Darts

Darts are one of the main means by which a piece of two dimensional fabric is turned into a three-dimensional shape; it can be given roundness or points as required.

The line of the dart may be straight, or in a convex or concave curve so transfer the dart markings from the pattern carefully with quick easily-removed tailor's tacks or chalk.

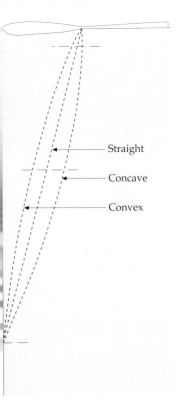

Straight
Concave
Convex

Press them well afterwards.

The seam allowances of deep darts in heavy fabric and those that are highly curved may need to be clipped.

Darts made on sheer fabric will need to be made with a double row of stitching and then trimmed and overcast.

Shirring and smocking

Shirring is created by making several rows of gathering. This might be done in ordinary thread and then gathered as required or by inserting shirring elastic onto the bobbin of the machine and gathering automatically as you sew.

In either case ensure the ends are oversewn well so that the gathering does not unravel.

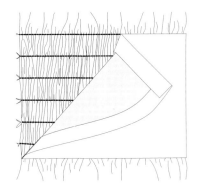

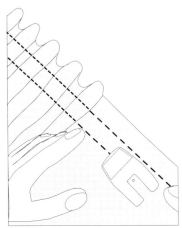

Shirring can be a quick way to gather in sun hats and mob caps and is great for 1940s-50s bathing costumes.

Smocking will provide a pretty decorative finish for many garments and is useful for children's clothes of many decades and yokels' smocks.

Shortcut smocking

Gather the fabric, running several parallel rows of stitching along the material, with shirring elastic wound onto the bobbin. Make sure the tension is not too tight or the elastic will snap–and ensure both ends are oversewn well and will not unravel.

Shirring looks effective just as it is but if you wish to add more colour and detail, thread embroidery silk through the machine stitching on the right side of material to make the smocking design required. Use loose embroidery stitches–cross stitch and feather stitch are fine for this as they are loose enough to 'give' sufficiently.

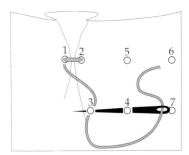

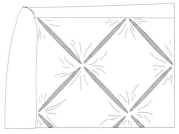

Machine hints

Stitch across pins, not along.

Make sure ends of stitching are well secured so the shirring cannot unravel again.

Check that the tension is not over-tight or the shirring will snap.

Fastenings

Fastenings for costumes in theatre use need to meet the following criteria:

They must be easy to do and undo as they will need to work smoothly when fast changes are required.

It is useful if they can be adaptable so as to allow costumes to fit more than one person.

It helps if the actor can dress or change without having to cry for assistance.

Zips

These are very versatile and easy to use, provided they are sewn in tidily and there are no loose threads to snag in the zipper workings.

However, if the costume is historical, they will need to be concealed. Zips were not invented until 1892.

It is easier to insert a zip smoothly if you ignore the pattern instructions and insert the zip before the garment is entirely joined together and the rest of the seam completed. It is much easier to work with two flat pieces of fabric than when everything else is in place and the seam already joined.

Buttons and buttonholes

Sewing on buttons is fairly straightforward. Use strong button thread and do the job thoroughly so that they will stand up to the strain of panic changes. Buttons can be a excellent decorative feature, whether functioning or not. It is possible to cheat, of course, and sew a button over another form of fastening such as a press stud or Velcro. Jewels or beads can be used as buttons.

Covering buttons can be effective, especially if the existing buttons on a garment are not right for the period.

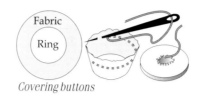

Covering buttons

Buttonholes can be created in many ways and are easier and quicker to do on machine than by hand. Use interfacing to reinforce lightweight fabrics.

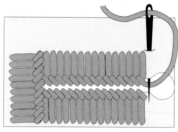

A handworked buttonhole can be finished with bar tacks and blanket stitch or have a keyhole finish.

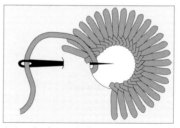

A circular buttonhole.

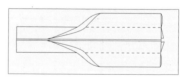

Whether machine or hand stitched use a fabric patch for fabrics that ravel or which are too heavy to simply stitch and slash.

Blanket or chain stitch can be used to create a button loop

Lacing

This provides a good period feel, for example, for medieval and Georgian bodices or back-laced Victorian underwear. Cord or tape, braid or ribbon can be used and the great advantage is that the costume can be adjusted to fit different sizes. The disadvantage is that it takes time to pull up and adjust!

Draw strings

These are especially useful because they can be tied to suit the particular neck or waistline. Ribbon or tape can be threaded through lace or a series of buttonholes in the fabric or through a seam and then tied as needed. This has the added advantage of allowing necklines to be raised or lowered to suit the character. Always ensure the ends cannot disappear into the fabric: tie knots or use toggles of some kind.

Rouleau loops

These look very pretty and give a good old-fashioned appearance.

Self-filled rouleau tubing

1 Make the rouleau tubing by stitching a bias strip with sufficient seam allowance to fill the tube when it is turned the right way out.

2 Sew through eye of a bodkin to material and then secure.

3 Pull bodkin and thread through tubing to turn this the right side out.

Cord-filled tubing

1 Cord can be threaded through a bias strip of fabric. Cut a piece of cord that is twice the actual length of the bias strip of fabric tube.

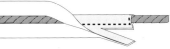

2 Stitch securely across the centre of the cording and then stitch the long edge of fabric.

3 Pull enclosed cord out of the tubing and this will turn the tubing the right side out and pull in the free cord.

4 Cut off the stitched end and any excess cording.

Rouleau tubing can be used as single individual loops or sewn in rows from one length of tubing to create button holes or lacing or a decorative feature. Attach so that the ends of the loops fall within the seam allowance of fabric pieces and/or facing.

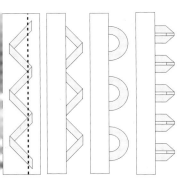

Frogs and balls

These can be made from braid or rouleau tubing and look good on uniforms, Napoleonic-style dress coats and Victorian and Russian clothes.

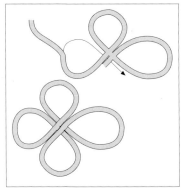

Use tiny stiches to hold the loops in place and to attach the finished frog. Complicated shapes can be basted on to paper before attaching to garments.

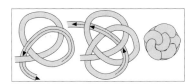

Small buttons can also be made.

Snap fasteners

These are quick and easy to attach and work well so long as the garment fits well or loosely and the fastening is not under stress!

The raised ball half should be attached to underside of flap and the socket on the garment section closest to the body.

Hooks and eyes

Hooks and eyes are secure and often used to catch the edge of a neckline, waistband, belt or cuff. They are fiddly to do in a hurry, however, and should be avoided for quick-change garments.

Velcro

Velcro is in effect a dense package of hooks and eyes that link when pressed together. It is very good for a fast change and can be used in side seams so that actors can easily leap in and out of costumes without assistance.

It is an excellent fastening device for hat straps and headbands (it might provide the basis for a crown or feather head-dress) cuffs, quick-change over-skirts and for optional removable accessories–such as lace trimmings and gauntlets, shoe decorations, belts and collars.

With Velcro such an invaluable asset in any theatre's wardrobe, conversation in the dressing room is often punctuated with the tearing noise of Velcro being peeled apart on all sides!

Pop rivets

A pop riveter or blind riveting tool is an excellent tool for making a very strong join of (or onto) heavy gauge materials. It can be used to fix fabric onto hardboard or metal, to join metal, leather, plastic and so on.

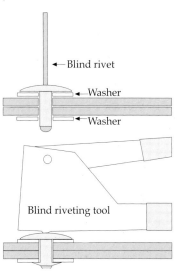

Blind rivet
Washer
Washer

Blind riveting tool

Ringing the changes: alterations and versatile garments

Creating your own stage costumes is often a matter of using materials and garments already in the wardrobe or bought in second-hand. Rarely is the small amateur company able to afford to purchase new fabrics for every costume in the play and creating costumes completely from scratch tends to be a luxury. So, while the costumier may be able to afford to make just one or two special dresses, generally the energies will need to be concentrated on alterations and adaptations. It is essential to know how to change costumes—to alter them to fit, to convert everyday garments into historical shapes or fantasy designs and to add decoration that transforms the commonplace into something exotic.

For reasons of economy and the future usefulness of any costume, it is also important to be able to make the costumes adaptable so that they can fit different sized performers and, with a little ingenuity, suit a variety of roles too.

Alterations

'I'll never fit into that!'

'It hangs off me!'

'I'm tripping up over the hem!'

'I wouldn't dare bend over!'

'I can't breathe!'

'It *sort* of fits . . .
but my hands have disappeared.'

Dealing with these problems is all part of the job! For major alterations it may be necessary to take apart the components of the costume and re-assemble them, as appropriate. The advice give here, however, is on how to make adjustments of a more temporary–and speedy–nature.

Prevention is better than cure - make costumes adaptable

When you make garments bear possible future adaptations in mind and take the following precautions!

Make sure the seams and hems are generous and not sewn so tightly that they are impossible to undo.

Whenever possible, make tops and skirts separately so that they will fit different combinations of figures and will be easier to adapt.

Skirts and waistlines should be elasticated: this will avoid a lot of problems. Draw strings can also alter the shape and fit of garments.

Using Velcro combined with a generous overlap of fabric will also create variable waistlines.

Look at the way handbags and soft luggage pieces are created to allow extra width to be absorbed when necessary. Some of these folds and tuck features can be absorbed into costume designs.

Drawstrings on waists and necklines mean these can be tied to suit the figure and the neckline can be as high or low as befits the role.

By using ribbon drawstrings, sleeves can also be worn long and flowing or long and gathered at the wrist, gathered above the elbow or three-quarters and puffed.

Fitting the figure

Adapting stage garments to make them wider is a common requirement and width can be provided, or reduced, in several ways:

Letting out or taking in the seams

If there are several seams, it is easiest to let out or reduce those with no fastenings or sleeve complications. However, it seems that whichever section you attack there are inevitably some complications. Altering width on the front or back pieces may affect waist seams, necklines—and zip fastenings, while side seam alterations may mean reinserting sleeves. Whatever you do, make sure the important seam lines still fall into the correct position on the actor.

Minor side seam alterations can be tapered away before the join with the sleeves is reached. In this way you can provide just a little ease without having to take out sleeves.

In the same way, small adjustments can be made to bodices or skirts without having to rework waistlines and necklines. The combined effect of these small alterations can often create sufficient extra inches.

If the seam is being taken in, a new seam can run from cuff to waist if necessary, provided the armhole curves are clipped.

Reducing or increasing the size of darts

This the simplest solution and can make a surprising difference. For example, if there are four darts around a bodice or skirt, by altering all of them a small amount, you may lose or gain a valuable inch or so.

Gussets

Gussets will be needed for more major letting-out alterations and you will need to find a fabric that blends in with the original. Actors and dancers use their arms a great deal and do not want to be caught mid-gesticulation by a tight armhole!

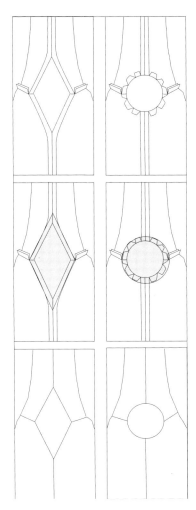

Diamond and circular gussets allow easier movement under the arm. Diamond gussets can also be set into waistline seams. Using a sash or wide belt afterwards can help to disguise these gussets.

Lace, tucks and ruffles

Lace fabric can be added in all sorts of places to provide extra width—or to disguise an extra seam that has been created to take up width.

Trim away underneath insertion and overcast raw edges. This is a very decorative way of lengthening a garment.

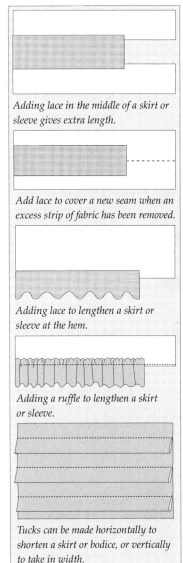

Adding lace in the middle of a skirt or sleeve gives extra length.

Add lace to cover a new seam when an excess strip of fabric has been removed.

Adding lace to lengthen a skirt or sleeve at the hem.

Adding a ruffle to lengthen a skirt or sleeve.

Tucks can be made horizontally to shorten a skirt or bodice, or vertically to take in width.

Trouble-shooting

Lengthening

Possible solutions	More information
Rehem: steam out any sharp folds and lines from the original hem and if necessary disguise resistant or faded lines with a trim of some kind.	Hemming stitch p28 Hems p32-3
Insert an extra panel right around the skirt, waistline, sleeve or trouser leg. Belts or sashes can disguise an extra waist panel.	Lace insertion p39, 49
Add a lace edging or some other trim around the bottom edge.	Lace, tucks and ruffles p39 Decorating p46-7

Shortening

Possible solutions	More information
Take up hems unless these are too large or too circular to adjust readily.	Hemming stitch p28 Hems p32-3
Horizontal tucks can also be created around a skirt–or sleeve–and make an attractive decorative feature.	Tucks and pleats p34
Lift shoulder seams.	
Raise or take in more at waistline.	Measuring up to adapt garments p24 Mix and match sizes p25

Tightening

Possible solutions	More information
Make more or increase size of original darts.	Dart sizes p25 Darts p35 Reducing p39
Create a series of tiny vertical tucks all the way around.	Tucks and pleats p34
Take in seam lines.	Seams p30-1 Taking in p39
Gather excess material and adjust (good for necklines and sleeves).	Machine p39 Alterations p38 Ruffling and rouching p34
Use elastic or shirring–good on circular or rounded seams.	Shirring p35
Move buttons and/or make new button holes, perhaps using rouleau or chain stitch loops.	Button holes p36 Chain stitch and rouleau loops p36-7

Loosening

Possible solutions	More information
Let out seams.	Seams p30-1 Letting out p39
Remove or reduce size of darts.	Dart sizes p25 Darts p35 Increasing p39
Use gussets.	Gussets p39
Add inserts of fabric or lace.	Lace insertion p39, 49
Loosen a neckline by drawing a line at the correct location, stay stitching and then clipping to this new seamline until comfortable. Then adjust the collar or facings to fit.	
Move buttons and/or make new button holes, perhaps using rouleau or chain stitch loops.	Button holes p36 Chain stitch and rouleau loops p36-7

Altering the appearance

The imaginative wardrobe mistress can see at a glance the possibilities of existing clothing. Bodices and skirts can be taken from different garments and made into one while the initial appearance of shape and fabric can be altered beyond recognition.

Ageing material

Combinations of the following may be used, depending on effect needed and how permanent this is required to be.

1 Wash garments to remove any sharply ironed creases.

2 Fade fabric with a bleach solution.

3 Use a cheese grater to wear away and fray edges.

4 Weigh down and steam pockets to sag.

5 Make shiny buttons or buckles dull with spray.

6 Dust in Fuller's Earth (this can be removed easily later).

7 Scrub clothes with a wire brush to distress the fabric.

8 Tear holes. Do not use scissors except to snip the inital cut.

9 Fray edges or make them ragged with a file or rasp.

10 Rub elbows and knees with candlewax untll they shine.

11 Make garment dirty with spray leather dyes, tempera paint, shoe polishes, and/or soil.

12 Apply pseudo caked-on dirt with a mix of glue, paint and sawdust.

13 Singe cut edges with an iron.

Batik

Batik can create very delicate or bold striking designs. Apply wax to areas that are not to be coloured. After applying paint or dye the wax is boiled off. This process can be repeated with various colours until the desired effect is reached.

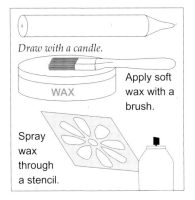

Draw with a candle.

WAX

Apply soft wax with a brush.

Spray wax through a stencil.

Dyeing

Dyeing will dramatically alter fabrics. Old sheets and blankets can suddenly take on a rich new look or, perhaps, a heavy dull one, depending on the colours chosen. Dying a whole range of costumes and fabrics is an excellent way of dressing a chorus in similar shades.

It is wise to test sample swatches first and of course, it is essential to check the instructions of commercial dyes properly and make sure you have the right dye for the fabric and the right quantities for the weight of material being dyed.

Small articles can be dyed in a pan on the stove but it is much easier to do large items in a washing machine.

Remember, you may need to fade out a strong colour first with a proprietary colour remover before trying to use a dye. Bleach can be used on some fabrics but never on silk or wool which will disintegrate.

Salt may be needed to fix the new colour. Check the dye instructions.

Natural dyes, such as tea and coffee, onions, onion skins, beetroot, crushed berries and walnuts can be fun to experiment with too. You will need some kind of mordant (a fix)–alum is good–and these dyes will work best on natural fibres like cotton and wool.

Tie dyeing produces lovely varied textile patterns. Wrap puffs and rolls of fabric in waxed thread or tightly gather and sew them. Dip them into dye to create random coloration. The material can be retied and redyed several times over.

Painting

Garments can be freely painted with fabric crayons and paint. This can be cheaper than buying braid or lace. Use a good hog's bristle brush if you want to apply dry paint or stipple.

Sketch in guide lines first: then use one or some of the following

Fabric paints

Designers' colours

Emulsion and acrylic paints

French enamel varnish

Shoe dye mixed with alcohol and shellac

Painting jewellery

Using glittery fabric paint is a quick way to create the effect of jewellery glowing on a garment or crown.

Sponging

Using a sponge (perhaps cut into an interesting shape) can allow a good deal of experimentation with colour as it builds up gradually.

Sprays

Sprays are simple to use and can alter fabric dramatically. Metallic and gold and silver sprays can be very useful. Always work near an open window and use a mask. Textures can be created by spraying through mesh.

Printing

Printing on fabrics can create interesting repeating patterns or borders. You can use potato cuts or wood or linoleum blocks. However, all of these printing skills require considerable

practice first before launching on to a finished garment or an expensive or valued fabric.

Screen printing

Screen printing is more sophisticated and needs special equipment. A thin sheet of film out of which the original design is cut is attached to mesh on a frame and the dye is forced through the screen on to the areas of garment not covered by the film. There may be a local expert who can help you or custom-make designs to suit the show's needs–such as tee-shirts with appropriate pictures and words.

Stencil printing

Stencil printing will create more controlled designs. Cut out separate stencils for each colour used from stiff oiled paper or thin shiny card, leaving plenty of surround. Stretch the fabric if it is elastic or gathered and make sure the paint is not too thin or it will dribble and not so thick that it stiffens the fabric.

Knitting and crochet or macramé work take longer than sewing but can be very useful if there is sufficient time. Perhaps you may be able to delegate a knitting project to a keen knitter in the group.

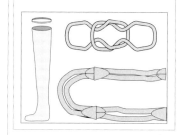

Chain mail and helmets can be made from knitted grey or black string or from cut nylon tights looped into lengths and then knitted. They can be sprayed with a metallic paint when finished. Garments already knitted up, such as old sweaters, can be cannibalized and made into chain mail vests if the edges are oversewn well, while balaclavas make a good base helmet.

Crocheted garments or tablecloths and upholstery articles may be found at flea markets and purchased for future use. Knitted shawls are a wardrobe 'standard' for historical plays of almost every period.

Spraying through mesh, or plastic fencing from a garden shop or waste from die cutting can give interesting results.

Lino cutting is difficult but a simple potato cut can be very effective.

Cut the stencil from stiff or oiled paper. You can use a spray, but a stencil brush will give you more control and interesting textures.

Mock leather

Making mock leather

You will need

Industrial felt

Lava soap

Brown acrylic paint

Brown shoe polish

Sponge

Scrubbing brush

To join the felt sections

Latex glue

or thonging cord
or brass fasteners
or metal eyelets and rivets
and a brawdall or punch to
make holes

1 First steam the felt to make sure it is sufficiently pre-shrunk.

2 Assemble the garment, using seams that are appropriate for the costume and period.

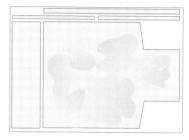

3 Rub the entire surface with lava soap, as patchily as possible.

4 Using a sponge, scrub in brown acrylic paint.

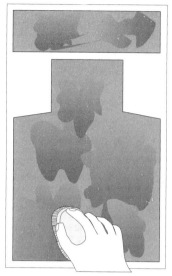

5 Leave to dry. Then rub in brown shoe polish and buff.

Making stiff 'leather' for armour

You will need

If making body armour
A tailor's dummy or one made up of cushions and foam

Aluminium foil sheeting or polythene to cover dummy

A wire frame for shaping helmets, shields and so on (Plastic bottles are good for leg guards)

Industrial felt

PVA (white flexible glue)
Or a size solution for small pieces of felt for gauntlets

Long T-pins or string

Shellac

Brown acrylic paint or shoe polish or bronze or black pigment in the final coat of shellac

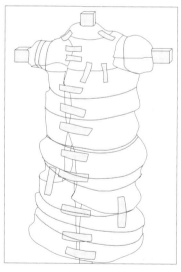

1 Pad a male dummy to size of actor. Cover with plastic or foil.

2 Cut felt to shape and then soak in a glue solution–2 parts PVA (white flexible glue) to 1 part water.

3 Pull and stretch the felt into shape on the mould and then pin or tie it into place.

4 Leave to dry for several days. Then remove from mould and apply a thin coat of shellac.

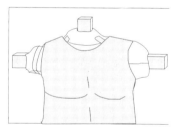

5 Decorate and paint as required. Pigment can be added to the final coat of shellac. Burnish to shine.

Creating shapes

Fantasy costumes for plays and pantomime are often three-dimensional shapes that need some inner support to hold the costume fabric in place.

Structures with wire or cane

Use a wire or hooped frame to form the basis of a large structure, such as a pumpkin or angel's wings.

Wire frames can also be used to make underskirts for crinolines. Hooped underskirts make very formal shapes but can be collapsed down once the garment is removed.

Shape-makers

All these can be used to make three-dimensional pieces. Basically, any rigid material will do so long as it is not too heavy to wear comfortably.

Stiff paper

Card and cardboard

Heavyweight interfacing

Stiffened fabric (sprayed or painted with PVA glue, shellac or equivalent)

Egg cartons

Corrugated cardboard

Polystyrene

Padding is needed to create rounded stomachs—and bustles.

Boning

Boning will be an essential part of many period costumes and underwear. Whalebone went out of use at the turn of the century and steel blades took their place. To protect the actor's tender skin, always use a continuous piece of boning that will stay in place and encase this between the fabric of a the garment and a twill strip or completely sandwich the bone first in two layers of fabric. Alternatively you can make a 'pocket' of tape on the garment and pop the bone inside before stitching across the top.

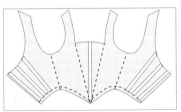

Stitched casings for bones in a corset.

Bone should be encased in layers of fabric or between twill tape and the fabric. Stitch carefully so the bones cannot work loose.

Liquid latex and shellac

◆ Liquid latex and shellac can be used to give body and rigidity to fabrics but do a patch test and check that the actor is not allergic to the substance if the garment is to be in immediate contact with the skin.

Here a papier maché head, hoops and a pole combine to give a fantasy costume rigidity and height.

papier maché

papier maché is excellent for making ...fer structures and can be made ...m wallpaper paste and paper, glue ...d cloth, size and paper, or flour and ...ter and paper.

...hichever constituents are used, the ...per will need to be torn up into irreg-...ar shapes or the cloth cut up into ...rips. Larger pieces can be used for ...ger structures but, generally, the ...aller the pieces, the better they will ...d together and the smoother the fi-...l finished surface.

...ways leave to dry in a well-ventilated ...om, and then paint with shellac or ...ulsion and seal, if required, with ...rnish or lacquer.

...wspaper, brown paper, tissue or toi-..., paper and kitchen towel paper can ...used. Generally, it is best to start ...h brown paper and then newspaper, ...llowed by tissue and toilet paper to ...eate a fine, smooth strong finish. ...wever, if you are making a mask or ...y item that will be in direct contact

---

---

with the skin, it might be advisable to begin with an inner layer of soft tissue to create a comfortable smooth surface on the inside.

Paper and wallpaper paste or PVA
1 Building on a frame, balloon, clay model or any existing object

1 Tear the paper into strips of various sizes. Do not use scissors.

2 Make up the wallpaper paste according to the instructions on the packet or dilute PVA with an equal amount of water.

3 Cover the frame with pieces of paper painted on both sides with your adhesive.

4 Now create a second layer. First add some paint to a small amount of adhesive. This will help you to see clearly the progress of the next layer and to ensure complete and even coverage of paper.

5 Continue creating layers of paper, using the coloured adhesive on alternate layers.

6 A small object will not need so many layers as will a large one such as a breast plate.

7 Finish with soft tissue paper torn into smaller pieces.

8 Leave to dry out thoroughly before decorating, preferably overnight.

Paper and wallpaper paste or PVA
2 Building a solid object

1 Tear the paper into strips of various sizes. Do not use scissors. Soak the paper in water.

2 Make up the wallpaper paste according to the instructions on the packet or dilute PVA with an equal amount of water.

3 Ring out excess water from paper and then immerse it in adhesive.

4 Crush and squeeze until paper is completely impregnated.

5 Squeeze out any surplus paste. Shape the pulp as if it is plasticine.

6 Mould it into the final shape required or, if it is an additional feature, apply it to the base object.

7 Leave to dry out thoroughly before decorating, preferably overnight.

Cloth maché

Glue and cloth maché creates sturdy pieces, useful for larger costumes.

Cloth and carpenter's glue or propriety wood adhesives

1 Cut cloth into strips, diagonally across the grain. Cheesecloth and canvas are good materials.

◇2 Make up the carpenter's glue: dissolve glue block or granules in a small bucket of water which is standing inside a larger metal bucket containing boiling water. Stir well and keep glue as hot as possible. Alternatively, the cloth can be soaked in PVA or proprietary wood adhesives that do not need to be heated.

3 Soak cloth strips in glue solution until completely impregnated.

◇4 Squeeze out any surplus glue (wear rubber gloves).

5 Apply cloth in overlapping strips to the mould or base until two or three layers thick .

6 Put some unsoaked paper into the glue solution and then apply in the same way. Use small pieces for the final layer to give a smooth finish.

7 Leave to dry out thoroughly before decorating, preferably overnight.

Decorating and finishing touches

Appliqué

Appliqué is basically separate shapes of fabric–hand or machine stitched to create designs and patterns on the surface of the fabric. Use fabrics that do not run, such as felt and polyester. Not only can plain garments can be given a fresh lift by decorating with appliqué but they can become something specific. The addition of stars and moons coverts a plain cloak into one that belongs to a wizard or magician.

Beadwork

Beadwork is excellent for giving a Victorian or 1920s look to a garment. Like sequins, they can be added singly, in a group or in a strand. You can string them yourself on a double strand coated with beeswax or on a nylon thread. Do not string them too tightly if you wish to make curves.

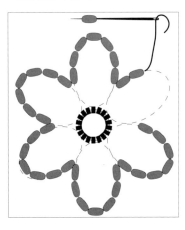

Bows

Rows of tiny bows or a single large one add an extra decorative flounce, particularly suitable for Victorian gowns and evening and wedding dresses.

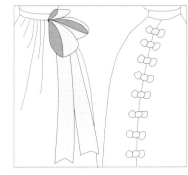

Creative embroidery

Creative embroidery will also add interest and detail but does take a long time to do by hand (see also page 29).

Feathers

Feathers add glamour to an ordinary hat or dress. To attach maribou trimming, make bar tacks for fabric loops about 4 inches (10cms) apart on right side of garment and thread the maribou through.

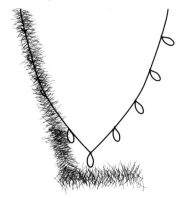

Fur

Fur trimmings (and accessories like fur hats and muffs) can add a nostalgic touch and suggest Edwardian skating scenes,1930s glamour or colder climates like Russia.

Lace and appliqué

Inexpensive place mats can be used create interesting cut-away designs.

Baste into position and then loop stitc into place. Trim away on the wror side, well within the stitched areas.

Gathered lace and ruffles are essenti for Regency and Edwardian style with roles like the Three Musketee and Prince Charming needing lavis frills and lace.

Machine stitching and embroider

Machine top stitching and embroider can be very effective and is muc quicker than hand stitching.

Organdie leaves and petals

Cut out petal shapes and stretch th fabric. Moisten your fingers in a bowl water and then roll up the edges . Thes delicate petals can be used to create single flower or a layered edging.

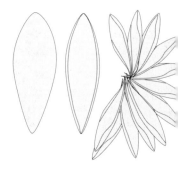

Patchwork

Patchwork is a good way to use up scraps of fabric effectively and is ideal for peasant and gypsy skirts and many kinds of ethnic skirts, shirts and tops. Patches make a skirt fit for Cinderella - and trousers for a tramp.

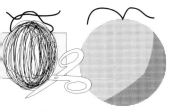

Pom-poms, tassels, and fringing

Pom-poms and tassels are made by winding wool around card.

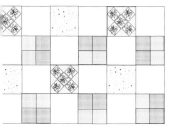

A fringe of tassels looks good on a Victorian shawl - while self fringing is a standard requirement for Wild West garments.

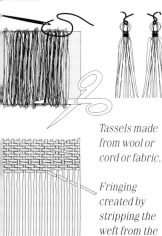

Tassels made from wool or cord or fabric.

Fringing created by stripping the weft from the warp of woven fabric.

Quilted fabrics

Quilted fabrics can be bought ready-made or created by pinning padding and backing to fabric and stitching through the layers to create squares, diamonds or stripes.

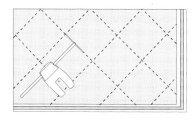

Quilting: corded

Corded quilting is a useful addition to Tudor and Elizabethan garments, especially sleeves and epaulettes or any item of clothing that will benefit from a ridged furrowed appearance. Creating thick ribbing by using rubber piping through material can be useful for alien or spacemen outfits.

Ribbons and braids

Trimmings decorate but can also alter a garment considerably and help it to take on new attributes. Braid will turn a plain blazer into a naval officer's uniform while ric-rac braiding is useful for gypsy boleros and skirts.

Make braid by plaiting cord, ribbon or rouleau tubing-maybe mixed colours.

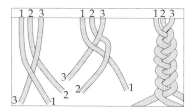

Make roses by twisting ribbon or braid.

Rouleau loops

Loops can be used for buttonholes or lacing, or as a decorative edging with narrow petersham or rouleau strips (see also pages 36-7) A continuous row of loops makes a pretty edging.

Sequins

Sequins can be sewn on individually or bought in bands of sequin trim on a fine backing foundation. They add instant glitter and glamour, especially effective under stage lighting.

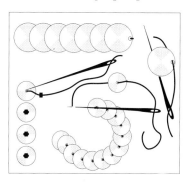

Smocking

Smocking gathers and creates folds that can make honeycomb, diamond or cable stitch patterns.

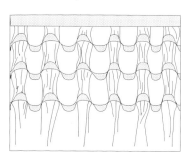

Re-cycling the wardrobe

Recognising the potential in everyday clothes and developing ideas on conversion and improvisation can save costs and be enormous fun.

It is particularly satisfying to hunt through the wardrobe and experiment with the existing resources, to envisage, for example, just how a change of neckline can convert a modest Victorian dress into a sexy one for a saucy Wild West barmaid!

Jewel   Scoop   U-neck

Bateau   V-neck   Square

Sweetheart   Keyhole   Halter

By the shirt tail!

Men's shirts are very adaptable garments, and cotton shirts are the best to use.

Stage costume is invariably attempting to revert back in time, and cotton fits the bill with its particular draping ability and matt surface texture. Added to these advantages, is the fact that cotton is easily dyed.

Polyester cotton is also a good fabric to use, although when dyed it remains light coloured and it impossible to achieve a deep colour dye. Nylon dyes well but its texture and shiny appearance is unsuitable for period pieces.

With the removal of the collar and the addition of frills and lace, men's white shirts can also be converted into Victorian blouses and pirate or Regency shirts.

To make a Victorian girl's smock

You will need

Man's white shirt; generous, not the 'slim-fit' kind

One pillowcase with a scalloped decorative opening edge or a length of broderie anglaise with a decorative border. This has to be two and a half times the width of the girl's shoulders (or the same width as the shirt if lengthening is required)

White bias binding

12 inches (30 cms) of narrow ribbon or three snap fasteners and three white buttons

To make base smock

1 Cut off the shirt sleeves, the complete collar, and the tails. Unpick and remove any pockets.

2 Hem or bias-bind the armholes and the neck.

3 Make a double row of running stitches along the shoulder seam. Gather to fit the actress.

The shirt is worn back to front!

To make yoke (using the pillowcase)

1 Cut off the decorative opening o the pillowcase, deciding on th depth of the material according t the size of the garment required.

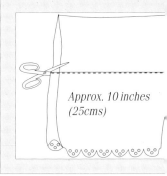

Approx. 10 inches (25cms)

To make yoke (using broderie anglaise)

1 Cut a length of broderie anglaise about 12 inches (30cms) deep.

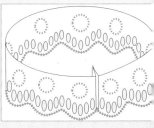

2 Join the ends together.

3 Hem the top and thread th channel this hem creates wit elastic that is loose enough to g over the head of actress.

The yoke should not be sewn on t the body of the smock because bot of these separate pieces, worn in dependently, might be useful o other occasions.

2 Undo the joining seams which join the front to the back.

3 Reassemble as illustrated: cut a central hole for the neck and leave the side open for pop fasteners, or buttons with ribbon loops.

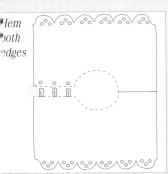

Hem both edges

4 Make ribbon loops to take buttons and attach as shown below.

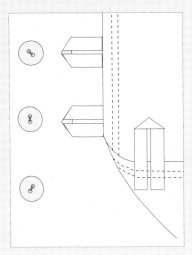

---

or example, the yokes could serve as a square Puritan collar or a round clown's ruff; and without the yoke, the smock could double up as a Victorian petticoat or a draped blouse in a Grecian drama.

Small cap sleeves can be added to the smock. Cut these from the tails of the shirt; their curved edges will be perfect and, as the outer edge is already hemmed, one process is eliminated.

4 Cut the shapes as shown and gather the raw edges.

5 Distribute the gathers across the shoulder seams of the shirt, allowing a distance of 4-6 inches (10-15 cms) to be covered.

6 Put the right sides of the shirt and cap sleeves together and stitch into position.

The surplus broderie anglaise left over after cutting out the yoke can be joined to the bottom of the shirt by one of the three following methods:

A Make a straight seam, with or without top stitching.

B Make a straight seam with top stitching and top-stitched 'tucks'.

C Use a lace insertion (see page 39).

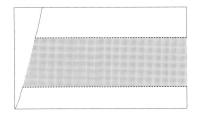

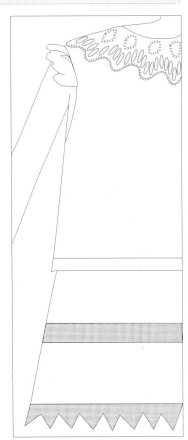

Various ways to use a circular piece of fabric

Keep life simple

A straight length or circle of fabric can often be contrived into an effective costume by judicious folding and a few simple seams. The costumier should always review a variety of approaches before launching into a complicated pattern–this may save precious time.

Up for conversion

Here are some further ideas for metamorphosis–mutating garments and household items to fulfil new roles!

Blankets: Rustic tunics, monk's habits, cloaks and capes.

Bedspreads: Ideal for wide skirts.

Curtains–net: Harem trousers, veils, fairy wings.

Velvet, chintz and brocade: Regency waistcoats and breeches.

Flip-flops, slippers and trainers: Can be converted into any manner of rustic and medieval shoes.

Fur coats–old: Animal costumes, hats, muffs, trimmings and cave men.

Lace doilies, antimacassars and tray cloths: Lace collars and cuffs, boot decorations, and shirt ruffles, small caps and aprons.

Leotards: These can have a wide variety of neckline styles and sleeve lengths and can be converted to suit tight-fitting tops or bodices from most periods as well as being a good base for an animal costume.

Nightdresses: Can be useful for making period underwear, Regency dresses or cut off to make blouses .

Rugs: Fur rugs or those with a cotton twist pile are good for animal costumes and for prehistoric man!

Sheets and tablecloths: Angel robes, Greek and Roman togas, pinafores and

Possible uses of a rectangular piece of fabric

aprons, cloaks, collars, full skirts and over-skirts.

Socks: Collect long men's socks as these are specially useful under breeches. Pulled over the top, mid-calf socks can make sneakers look like boots or shoes.

Stockings and tights: Heavy gauge ones are very useful for men's clothing, especially dark ones and almost any weight white ones for 18th-century costume.

Ordinary tights can be a useful filler for stuffing articles like crinoline and shoulder pads and can be knitted together to make a coarse fabric or chain mail.

Sweaters - polo-neck: The fine smooth kind can be dressed up with braid and buttons for 16th-17th century men's tops.

Towels - bath: Good source of fabric for tunics, turbans, cloaks, old-fashioned bathing costumes, biblical robes.

Track-suit bottoms and ski pants: Chop off short to make Regency breeches; criss-cross with cord around the calves for medieval ones.

Travelling rugs: Sherlock Holmes style cape coats, Victorian skirts.

Trousers - men's: Chop them off at the knee to make breeches for almost any historical period from the middle ages onwards. Try gathering them around the ankles and at the waist to turn them into farmer's or peasant's trousers.

Accessories

Hats

Hats are a vital part of any costume. Such is the enormous impact of a hat that impersonators often rely on them as the sole change of costume required—all that they need to denote a new personality.

Of course, a wide choice of headgear can be borrowed, albeit at a price, from theatrical costume hire companies but it is much more fun to make your own or to adapt existing hats. Old hats can generally be found in abundance in jumble sales and charity shops and are usually relatively cheap to buy second hand. Ask if the cast have any.

Actors need to be seen

Do remember, whatever the style of hat, that the actor's face needs to be seen. Big brims cast shadows over the face and profiles can all too easily be concealed by hats—and hair. Do not add to this problem or the actor will have to find an excuse to remove the hat almost immediately.

Millinery basics

There is no need to be a fully fledged milliner in order to make hats for a production but it may help to have some notion of the basics, even if only as a guideline when altering existing hats.

Materials

Stage headgear can range from a pirate's head scarf to a king's crown made of cardboard, an inverted wastepaper bin covered in paper flowers, a fur hood, a white Puritan bonnet or a mesh hairnet that might suggest a medieval lady or one from the 1930s. Simply because there is so much variety, stage hats can be made from virtually any material suitable to the specific hat. As with other dressmaking for theatre, an imaginative approach will often serve better than rushing out to buy precisely what a pattern dictates—if indeed you can find an appropriate pattern in the first place!

However, to mould a new shape, straw and felt are best. These materials (or old hats made of them) can be stretched over a curved surface, (preferably a proper head block) pinned and treated with steam, heat and pressure to force them into shape.

Use natural fabrics rather than synthetic ones if you wish to block a shape. Materials that can be blocked include:
straw
felt
cottons
denim
linen
velvet
wool fabrics
jersey

Hats that are to be cut from a flat pattern, rather than blocked, can be made from almost any material that is not too heavy or stiff, such as:
canvas
cotton
chintz
corduroy
denim
fur fabric
leather and suede
PVC
satin
silk
tweed
velvet and velour

Hats can also be knitted . . .

Or made by origami—folding strong paper or material

Or made from ordinary household items like lampshades and boxes

Or made from polystyrene

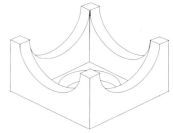

Or from sponge covered with material

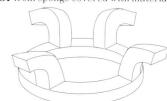

Or from papier maché—ideal for creating novelty shapes when built up around a balloon, over a wire mesh frame, or inside a plastic plant pot or a cake tin.

Hat terminology

Brim

Crown

Head ribbon
or band

Peak

Sectional
crown

Tip

Side band

Head fitting

Under brim

Ladies - some hat types and shapes

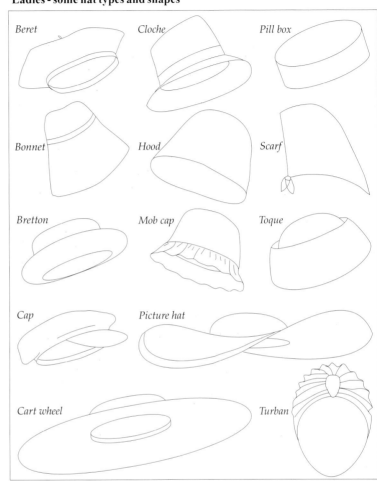

Beret

Cloche

Pill box

Bonnet

Hood

Scarf

Bretton

Mob cap

Toque

Cap

Picture hat

Cart wheel

Turban

Mens

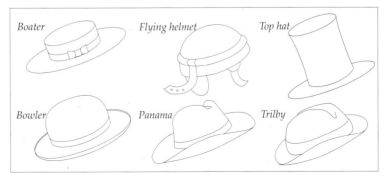

Boater

Flying helmet

Top hat

Bowler

Panama

Trilby

*From these basic shapes, other hats,
such as a cowboy's Stetson or a
sultan's turban can be created.*

Measurements and sizes

A basic hat measurement is taken right around the head, just above the eyebrows. To fit a head-hugging style you will need to measure across the top of head from ear tip to ear tip and from the forehead to nape.

Hat sizes chart

Hat size	inches	mm
5 7/8	18 3/4	476
6	19	483
6 1/8	19 3/8	492
6 1/4	19 3/4	502
6 3/8	20 1/2	521
6 1/2	20 3/4	527
6 5/8	21	533
6 3/4	21 1/4	540
6 7/8	21 5/8	549
7	22 1/4	565
7 1/8	22 1/2	572
7 1/4	23	584
7 3/8	23 3/8	594
7 1/2	23 3/8	603
7 5/8	24	610
7 3/4	24 1/2	622
7 7/8	25	635
8	25 1/4	641

Shape of head opening.

Stiffening

Hats may be stiffened with straw varnish, felt stiffener or Feltene varnish painted on after steaming. Many other fabrics can be stiffened by spraying with proprietary stiffeners, such as those supplied for turning fabric into roller blind material.

Millinery wire (this is a wire covered in fine cotton thread,) can be used to make a headband or to firm up the edge of a brim.

Interlinings of various weights, such as Vilene, can also be used between layers of fabric—as can cardboard but cardboard does not have the resilience to stay looking good for very long, especially if it is bent or if the hat gets wet! Buckram can be used to make a stiff inner frame for a hat.

> **Tools**
> Pliers
> Scissors
> Craft knife
> Kettle
> Tailor's chalk
> Thimble
> Dressmaker's pins
> Drawing pins
> Sewing machine
>
> **For shaping hats**
> Wooden crown block
> Brim block

Alternatively, a simple pressing pad might be used. This can be just a wad of cotton folded over lots of times.

If it is thick enough and you are very careful, this wad can be used in the hand when you are shaping material.

Blocking felt or other suitable fabric

1 If the material is thin or is to be stretched a good deal, paint some stiffener on to the inside of the 'hood'. Allow the stiffener to dry out completely.

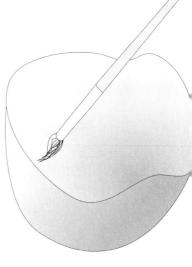

5 Cut away any surplus. A light steaming and a brush will raise the pile of felt.

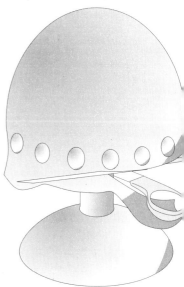

2 Cover the block with cling film or plastic wrap to avoid any dye staining that might spoil the next hat you make.

3 Allow steam to penetrate the material for about five minutes.

4 Stretch the material over the block and pin it into place with good quality drawing pins or tie in place with a length of cord.

 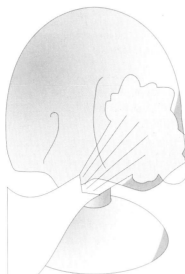 

6 Brims can be stretched and shrunk to fit a special brim block or steamed and stretched, using a damp cloth and an iron or kettle or shaped by hand.

7 If the crown and brim have been shaped separately, they will need to be joined together with large back stitches.

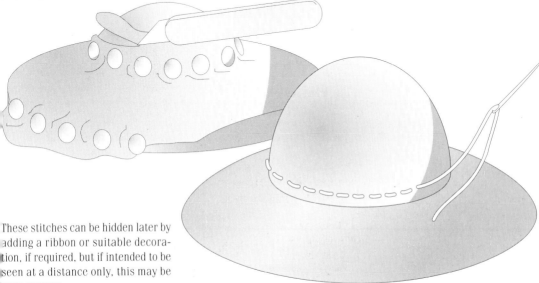

These stitches can be hidden later by adding a ribbon or suitable decoration, if required, but if intended to be seen at a distance only, this may be unnecessary.

Converting existing hats

Converting existing hats

A conventional plain hat can be altered dramatically by simply bending, cutting, or folding.

A round felt hat becomes an 18th-century tricorne hat.

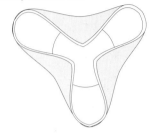

Feathers–large feathers turn a lady's hat into a cavalier's.

17th-century Puritans.

A straw hat tied with a scarf becomes a bonnet shape.

Decoration of hats

A plain hat can be decorated with any of the following:

Bear in mind that minute details will not be seen by an audience so be as flamboyant as befits the character.

Appliqué

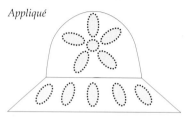

Artificial fruit

Beads

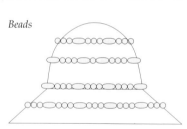

Belt and buckles

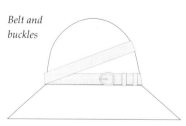

Braid

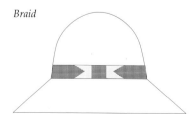

Buttons

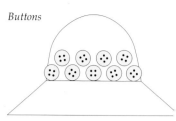

Chiffon

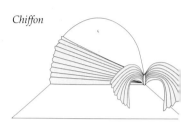

Embroidery by machine or hand

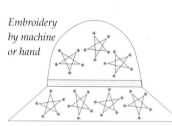

Feathers

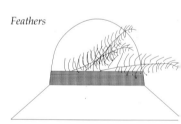

Flowers

Hair can also be added–this might be ringlets tumbling from a bonnet or a netted wig below a wimple, or plaits attached to a Dutch winged hat. Extra hair can be especially useful for witches or wizards when strands of wild tangled wool or grey locks look very effective.

Making simple hats

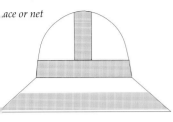

Lace or net

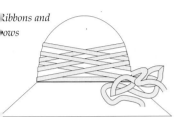

Ribbons and bows

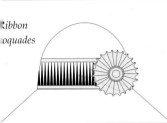

Ribbon cocquades

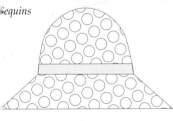

Sequins

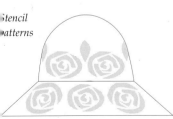

Stencil patterns

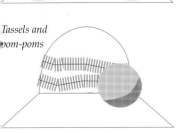

Tassels and pom-poms

A simple top hat or stove hat

This can be made from card, felt glued onto cardboard, or sized material–or from fabric that has been stiffened with blind stiffener or lined with something that is rigid enough to retain the shape of the 'stove'.

1 Cut out brim, side and crown. Allow a good 3cm (1¹/₆ins) seam.

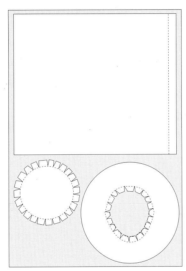

2 Clip to the seam line of both crown and inner edge of brim at regular intervals, as shown.

3 Join the edges of the upright cylindrical section.

4 Stitch or glue the tabs into position to join the crown on to the upright section, making sure the tabs are located inside the hat.

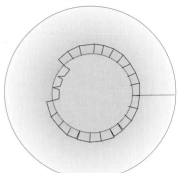

5 Stitch or glue the tabs into position to join the brim on to the upright section, making sure the tabs are located inside the hat 'stove'. Any unsightly seams can be hidden with suitable tape or braid.

6 Making a larger brim and a smaller crown and tapering the cylinder will turn the top hat into a 17th-century shaped hat for Guy Fawkes or an American Puritan.

A simple bonnet

Like the top hat, this can be made of card or suitably rigid material. Simply cut out one of each section–a back (A), a central arched piece (B) and a brim (C). Join them together as described in steps 6-8 below.

Alternatively, ordinary fabrics like cotton can be used–provided this is lined as described here.

1 Cut out one back(A), one central arched piece(B) and two identical brims (C).

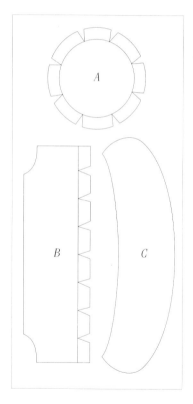

2 Cut out one A, one B, and one C in stiff Vilene.

3 Stitch or iron on the Vilene (as appropriate) to the wrong side of one A, one B, and one C.

4 Keeping the right sides together, sew together the two brims (C), leaving a gap.

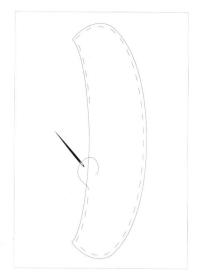

5 Turn the brim the right side out and oversew the unstitched edge.

Now you have stiffened sections ready to join together to make the final hat.

6 Clip the edges of A and B.

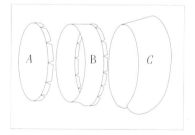

7 Join the slashed edge of the arched section into a circle and insert the circular back crown section into this. Stitch or glue together, as appropriate.

8 Attach the brim to the front of the arched section, gathering as necessary to fit.

Scarves

There are all sorts of ways that scarves can be used to make headgear and suggest character.

Tying a scarf in various ways–for a charlady ... and a pirate

Making crowns

There are many different kinds of crown and coronet that have graced the heads of high ranking nobility and sovereigns right around the world throughout the centuries. Pantomime and fairy stories, nativity plays, Shakespeare performances, historical productions and pageants are all likely to need the odd crown or two.

Many of these crowns might well be decorated with sequins, jewels, or other such blandishments. The section on jewellery on pages 65-6 provides some useful ideas.

Here are a few suggestions on how to make crowns:

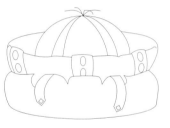

Simply join together two brightly coloured soft felt hoods. Decorate with strips of contrasting felt, ribbon or braid. Roll up the edges—which can then be slashed and 'castellated'.

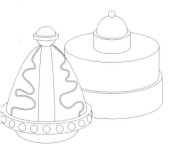

Felt can be blocked into pill-box, cones or pyramid shapes and then decorated imaginatively.

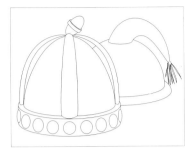

Straw sections from the centre of straw sun hats can be used as a basis for a fez or small crown.

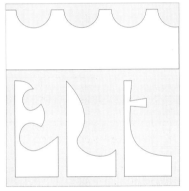

Shapes like this should be placed on a fold and cut out twice.

The simplest crown of all is made from card which is cut and glued. Gold or silver spray, glitter or gleaming foil paper add an extra sparkle.

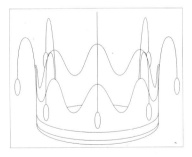

Stiff material such as buckram or felt lined with Vilene can be given extra rigidity by using wire struts which can be bent into curves and decorated.

Crowns can be decorated with braid, piping, cord and string, fur, pearls and buttons and almost any regular shapes cut, painted or sprayed.

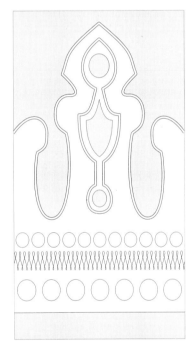

Using household items

Hats can be made from everyday articles. For example you might wish to convert a straw refuse basket, a plastic flower pot or a lamp shade—with or without the addition of a brim. Fibrous planters and liners for hanging baskets might make useful bases too.

Create a hat from a lampshade

In this instance a lampshade base has been used which, once covered, may be suitable as a base for a fantasy hat. A large brim can be added and this, along with suitable decoration, could serve as a dame's bonnet or an oversized 'cartoon' character's hat. Alternatively the basic hat, turned upside down and decorated, could make a very impressive crown.

1 Bind the circular struts with narrow, straight binding tape.

2 Pull the fabric taut and pin the side seam, lining it up with one of the vertical struts.

3 Remove fabric, machine side seam, trim off surplus, and fit back on to frame, right side out.

4 Roll the spare material at top and bottom around the two circular struts. Stitch this fabric into position, catching the fabric on to the binding.

For a pleated frame

1 Bind the circular struts with narrow, straight binding tape.

2 Stitch the side seam. You will need to angle this according to the shape of the frame.
(For very flared frames, use two seams to avoid fabric wastage.)

3 Replace the fabric over the frame, right side out.

4 Pin gathers evenly around the top of the frame.

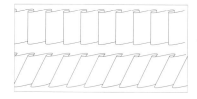

5 Repeat at the base, distributing the gathers to make the pleating follow the same direction, slanted or vertical, as shown above.

6 Oversew the gathers into position, neatly catching the binding with the thread.

A basic beret

1 Cut out a circle of fabric for the beret's crown and a length of fabric for the headband.

2 First make the headband. Simply fold the headband piece into a circle, right sides together. Join the two short ends as shown.

3 Turn right side out. Fold the headband piece in half, lengthways, with the wrong sides together.

Turn in the rough edges. Tack up these edges or press well with an iron.

4 Sew around the circumference of the crown with running stitches.

5 Gather the edge of the crown to fit the headband and then attach crown to headband, ensuring the rough edge of crown is tucked into the headband.

6 Topstitch to secure crown edges within headband.

7 Several rows of top stitching will give the headband extra rigidity.

This basic beret can be altered dramatically by changing the sizes of the crown and depth of the headband.

A mob cap

1 Cut out a circle of fabric, with a minimum diameter of 610mm (24 ins). Make little clips at regular intervals around the edges to allow the curved edges to turn in easily.

2 Turn in the edges and add a trim of lace or broderie anglaise.

3 Gather the hat with sheering elastic.

Or attach a narrow circular strip of bias fabric or bias binding to the inside of the hat and thread elastic through this to gather the hat.

This kind of cap serves as a bed cap, serving wench's cap, or a Victorian bathing hat.

Chinese 'castle' hat

1 Cut out the six segments and a fairly wide hat band.

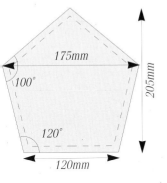

2 Make the hat band as described in the beret instructions (page 60).

3 Join the six segments together.

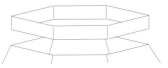

4 Attach the hat piece to the headband, making sure the back seam of the band matches up with one of the segment seams.

5 Hand sew a tassel onto the centre of the hat.

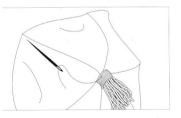

A baseball or school boy type cap

This is made in a similar way to the castle hat but with six curved pieces and with the addition of a stiffened peak. It does not have a fabric headband but is generally lined and has a headband made of petersham set inside the cap. The addition of ear pieces turns this into a flying cap or, if made in tweed, into a Sherlock Holmes hat.

Sultan's turban

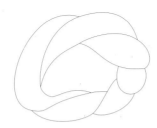

Create a sultan's turban by making two sausages of fabric filed with wadding. Twist these sausages together, intertwining them with strings of pearls.

Gloves

During the sixteenth and seventeenth centuries, gloves for both men and women became an integral part of the fashions of the time, and have continued to change in length to suit the rise and fall of the sleeves ever since.

Since gloves are rarely worn these days they have an immediate effect on the stage and make the actors feel different too—whether they are elegant long satin evening gloves or the fingerless woollen mittens of an old tramp. They can be difficult to get used to, especially if the actors have to conduct any delicate procedures with their begloved hands so it is best to wear them early on in rehearsal. Try to build up a collection of gloves of every length and in a good variety of colours and materials—leather, linen, satin, lace, wool. Many gloves can be used just as they are but some may be useful for converting into gauntlets.

If you can, find gloves that can be washed so that they are not spoiled by make-up. Kid gloves can be washed gently in soapy water and, if very old and spotty, may be dyed in weak coffee or tea solution. Store gloves carefully in bags or in pocketed hanging 'tidy bags' as any such tiny items are easily lost, especially in the whirl of quick changes during a production. A tidy bag is useful for storing small items such as gloves and jewellery.

Making gauntlets

Conventional men's gloves can be easily turned into gauntlets by adding leather extensions or a stiffened piece of fabric cut and stitched as shown below. Try to choose a stiffening that is washable, such as canvas or Velcro. A lace addition will turn the glove into a cavalier's gauntlet.

An old cycling glove can be changed into an armoured gauntlet for a knight by gluing string around the fingers, adding a cone-shaped cardboard gauntlet and then applying metallic paint or spray.

Cut two gauntlet pieces and join them together. Spray or paint fabric or stiffen with a (preferably washable) lining.

Line up the less flared seam of the gauntlet with the side of the glove nearest to the thumb and then attach gauntlet at the wrist.

Adding an 'extention' to the glove changes it into a gauntlet.

Shoes, boots and bags

Actors come in all shapes and sizes—and so do their feet. Shoes can be collected from the usual jumble sale and charity shop sources and will often be donated once the word is out that you will welcome their arrival. They can be scrubbed and polished or brushed and then bagged up in types and or size. They are bulky and awkward to store—which is why people are often happy to give them away to you —but very useful if you have room.

Improvisation, decoration and dyeing

Dying, painting, spraying and decorating can turn old court shoes, boots and pumps into very useful additions to the wardrobe. There are lots of proprietary brands available and even a different shoe polish will provide a darker tone as a temporary measure.

1 First remove any old dye with a deglazing fluid.

2 Stuff shoes with newspaper to retain shape.

3 Apply new spray colour, building up layers as required to create correct depth of colour or to mix colours and create a new shade.

4 Apply paste wax and buff gently with a soft cloth.

Use your imagination. Look at the potential of what is available in the wardrobe and first analyse the general shape of the shoe you wish to emulate—the length and curve or point of the toe shape, the heel shape and height, how high the front comes up the foot and what shape this is too.

Then decide whether there are straps or laces or bows. Once this is established, it is surprisingly easy to find existing shoes with the same basic style and to adapt them, adding features and detailing to suit the period.

For decoration, collect old belts and buckles, buttons, fabric bows, jewellery, toggles, spurs—even budgerigar or cat bells!

Greek, Roman or Biblical sandals

Flat-heeled leather sandals or espadrilles may look quite acceptable. Otherwise a rope sole or a flip-flop can be converted by adding leather or string thongs.

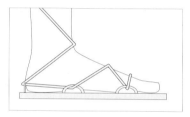

Alternatively buy shoe 'socks' or liners of the appropriate size. Use these as a template and cut out surrounds, about an inch wider all round, from industrial felt or layers of heavy-gauge stiff fabric. Stick the shoe liners onto the surrounds. Make loops of tape and thread thonging through these.

Middle Ages footwear

Dark socks can be pulled right over the top of sneakers or flip-flops to look like soft medieval shoes. Tie leather straps or thongs around legs. Alternatively, you can cut out and gather ovals of felt.

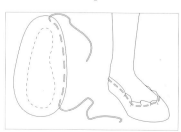

15th-century or oriental shoes

Pointed medieval shoes can be made felt. These may be turned into orient. slippers by curling up toes with wir. You will need some heavy-gauge fel and some pliable wire that is firm enough to retain its shape but not to brittle and not so heavy that it hurts th wearer's feet.

1 Cut out a shoe sole . Drawing round the actor's foot will provide a template but remember to allow a good margin for seams and to add about 8 inches (20 cm) tapering to a point, beyond the toes.

2 Cut out two sides and one top gusset piece. Cut two pieces of wire that are just less than the length of material along the long sides of the top gusset. Cover wire with fabric, allowing a good seam clearance. Attach fabric-covered wire by sewing to the inside of the top gusset sides.

3 Join the two side pieces together at the back, wrong sides together.

4 Attach the 'wired-up' top gusset to the side pieces, wrong sides together, and then join this top section to the shoe sole by oversewing.

5 Twist the wire at the point of the shoe into a curve. Add a bell or tiny pom-pom to tip, if required.

8th-century shoes

ry adding buckles or bows to ladies'
ourt shoes and mules–and buckles on
o men's shoes. Add felt tops to boots.

Victorian boots

dd spats with buttons or laces to turn
ourt shoes into dainty boots.

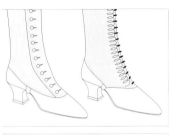

Shoe conversions

*Modern men's shoes can be
converted with the addition of felt
tongues and buckles or thick felt
cuffs can be added to boots.*

Bags

Bags are a vital part of an outfit and,
like shoes, can be bought up and stock-
piled, dyed, decorated and altered to
suit requirements.

Simple 'makes'

Purses have been used by men and
women to carry money and small be-
longings up until the 15th century
when pockets became commonplace.
They might be worn about the waist, often attached to a belt–or sometimes
around the wrist.

Simple purses and bags of all sizes can
be made by creating a square or oblong
pouch of material and then threading
cord through the top seam, leaving a
gap for the cord to protrude and form
both a drawstring and a handle. Made
of almost any material, such as leather,
cotton or velvet, a simply styled bag
can be suitable for a huge variety of periods and lifestyles, depending on the
choice of fabric and decoration.

A round purse

1 Cut two circles of fabric and join
right sides together, leaving a gap
for turning right side out. Slip stitch
the unsewn 'opening'.

2 Make evenly spaced eyelet holes
around the perimeter.

3 Thread two drawstrings in and out
of the eyelet holes, starting at
opposite sides to create one loop on
each side. Pull drawstrings to close.

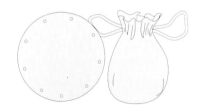

Alternatively, make a round bag from a
circular base, firmed up with cardboard, and an oblong strip of fabric
joined into a cylinder shape and then
gathered at the top.

Satchel-shaped bags and purses can
be made by cutting out material as
shown here, and then saddle stitching
or machine stitching the edges together. Greater depth can be created by the
addition of a long strip between the
front and back. Straps and buckles can
be added. Old belts may be usefully
chopped up for this!

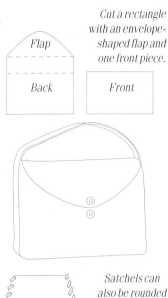

*Cut a rectangle
with an envelope-
shaped flap and
one front piece.*

Flap

Back

Front

*Satchels can
also be rounded
and saddle
stitched.*

Umbrellas and parasols

Although used in Egypt 3000 years ago, probably as a ceremonial object a well as to protect regal heads from the sun, umbrellas and parasols did not really appear in general use until the mid-eighteenth century and were initially the subject of much scorn and ridicule. In time, however, parasols became increasingly popular until they were a prerequisite part of the apparel for the fashion-conscious mid-nineteenth century lady.

Once again, let the scavenging instinct loose: scour the jumble sales, junk stores and charity shops for unloved umbrellas and parasols. These can be recovered in suitable fabric, if necessary. Alternatively, parasol frames can be purchased from costume or novelty companies and then covered to suit your needs.

To recover an umbrella or parasol, remove the old material carefully and use this as a pattern. Lay the old pieces on fresh fabric and cut out new sections. Machine stitch sections together.

Making sure the seams line up with the spokes, secure the new cover at top and bottom of each spoke, stretching the material tightly.

Fringes, lace, ruffles and braid can be added but do be careful to check that the parasol still opens properly. Keep checking this as the trim is added.

For oriental parasols, use a circle of strong patterned paper. Fold in half with the wrong sides together. Open up circle. Fold in half again. Repeat until you have either eight or sixteen creases with the wrong sides together. Then make another set of folds, with the right sides together, alternating with the original creases, to create a zig-zag effect .

Alternate folds crease in opposite directions.

Jewellery

general plea amongst the cast will usually provide a good starting point for the group's jewellery collection. From that point on, it can be difficult to refrain from accumulating more and more as the variety of old brooches, necklaces and ear-rings to be discovered can turn the enthusiastic costume hunter into an avid collector.

Much of the jewellery that is unearthed locally at a rational price will be fairly tatty. However with ingenuity, spray, new threading and care and attention, even really tired old things can, just like some of the actors and actresses, be given a new lease of life and look really gorgeous seen at a distance under the lights!

Making your own

This can be a real challenge and lots of fun. Almost anything that can be strung, glued, painted, sprayed, sewn, and brought together can provide a cheap source of exotic-looking jewellery with the application of some creative and imaginative attention.

Home and garden and do-it yourself

When television viewers watched the award-winning *The Six Wives of Henry VIII* several decades ago, most of them were unaware that the brilliant jewellery which encrusted the bodices and sleeves of the Tudor garments was, in fact, created from dried foodstuffs like lentils and from nuts and bolts—suitably coloured and varnished of course!

It can be highly profitable to search through the tool stores for useful washers, rivets, eyelet's, nuts and bolts, springs, rods, metal and plastic tubes, ball bearings, chains, spiral bits and S-hooks. Cleaned and, if required, sprayed a gleaming gold, ruby, emerald or copper they will provide wonderful ornament. Metal sink grates make a good brooch base.

Other good materials
Balsa wood
Leather
Sheet metal
Shells
Wire
Wood

Then attack the food stores for spaghetti and macaroni, dried peas, split peas and so on which can also be transformed with similar treatment.

The next place to hunt is the office for polystyrene shapes, treasury tags, tin-tacks and so on—and then the sewing drawer for buttons (especially pearl or gilt ones), zipper tags, tassels, braid, press studs, beads, curtain rings and so on. Lace can be stiffened and then painted or sprayed.

Seeds can also be very interesting shapes so look in the garden and garden stores too. Apart from the obviously rounded lupin seeds, oval melon and sunflower seeds, acorns and beans, do not overlook fascinating poppy heads and hollyhock whorls.

Bamboo sticks can be cut and threaded and small pebbles may be painted and glued while the gravel from fish bowls will provide tiny stones.

These pieces can, as appropriate, be attached on to buckram, felt, braid, leather, or ribbon, or to brooch or tie pins. They might be pierced into Perspex or wood, joined with metal links or linked on to chains, strong thread, wire or metal strip. They can be threaded, hooked on to ear-ring fittings—or on to any of the proprietary fittings available in haberdashery, craft or bead shops.

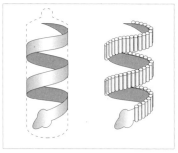

Ancient style bracelets can be cut out of a plastic bottle, glued with cut straws and given a metallic spray.

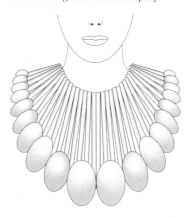

Straws can be glued on a fabric or card base and painted or sprayed. Add nuts and bolts, buttons or foil.

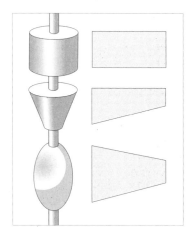

Paper spiralled into beads around a lubricated knitting needle can be threaded into necklaces or bangles.

Hot melt glue guns are useful for applying decoration, especially gold and silver leaf. Dullcote spray enamel will create a matte finish while Rub and Buff will lessen shine and suggest age.

Fimo, baked in the oven, can be a very versatile material for purpose-made jewellery. It can be shaped like plasticine and coloured precisely to suit the costumier's needs.

Watches and Spectacles

While collecting together jewellery do not forget to gather in old watches. These were first worn by men in the late sixteenth century. Large-face watches make useful fob watches for Victorian and Edwardian gentlemen while smaller ones for ladies should be hung on dainty chains around the neck for the nineteenth century or made up as pins or brooches for 1900-1918. Wristwatches were introduced just before the First World War. Plain watches can be pinned onto a nurse's uniform. Remember digital watches did not appear until the 1960s.

Spectacles were not really invented until 1727. Pince-nez appeared in the 1840s while the lady's lorgnette was very popular in the early nineteenth century. As well as the usual 'junk' sources, ask opticians if you can raid their old stock to establish a good range of different shaped spectacles. It is useful to collect some spectacles without lenses as glass reflects stage light and can look strange—sometimes this may be a desirable effect to establish character. Plain glass can be used but do not expect actors to stumble about wearing prescription lenses that make them unbalanced and dizzy!

a) Decorate felt. card or buttons with seeds, string or beads.
b) Bracelets can be made of card or stiffened felt moulded over a tin can in two hinged halves that will later clip together with Velcro or press studs.
c) Paper doilies or real lace can be sprayed or painted.
d) Discs of felt, leather or card can be theaded over elastic or braid; Curtain rings can be thonged together or linked—with tiny leather bands stitched around or with S-hooks.
e) Metal tubes and rods or macaroni and spaghetti can be made into interesting ear-rings and necklaces.

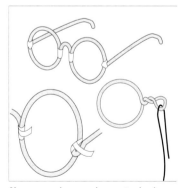

You can make pseudo spectacles by twisting fine gauge wire. Protect sharp ends well and hold joints with tape.

Other accessories and trimmings

Fans

Fans can be made from silk, paper, wood, bamboo, plastic, lace, fabric and feathers and in the early 1400s were originally stiff, not folding as we know them today. Folding fans arrived in 1549, first appearing in the Paris court in the hand of Catherine de Medici.

The two outer sticks are thicker than the inner ones and are generally more decorative. The working folding fan is complicated to make but open ornamental ones and concertina oriental paper versions may fall within the scope of the amateur. It is, of course, possible to recover a fabric fan or to decorate an existing one. Fans can also be hired from specialists in this field.

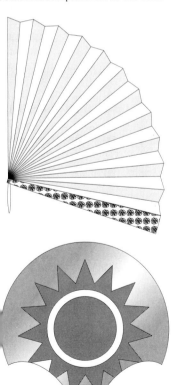

Adding an extra flourish

Flowers from fabric

Quite often a simple dress or an outfit needs a 'lift', or maybe the script calls for a dozen red roses (out of season!). Perhaps the leading lady's hat looks more suitable for a funeral than for a wedding–on such occasions artificial fabric flowers will solve the problem.

These flowers are really quite expensive to buy (especially when more than the odd one is required), and even then the correct flower or colour cannot always be purchased. Home-made fabric flowers are surprisingly inexpensive to make and, of course, the range of blooms and colours is far greater than those found in shops.

Not only are these flowers useful for garments, hats, and for bouquets but they are equally useful on the 'props front'. You can be guaranteed 'wilt-proof' blooms for each performance! Gone are the days when you have to chat up a local florist to provide daily blooms for your production. (Also bear in mind that real flowers on the stage may be regarded as bad luck!)

An enormous variety of blooms can be made from a wide assortment of fabrics. Within reason most materials can be used. The main criteria is that the fabric will hold its moulded shape once starched. Try to match the texture of the fabric to that of the flower to be copied. Some textures lend themselves to particular blooms; for instance, silk (man-made or natural) and satin will make both splendid roses, whereas crinkle cotton is more suitable for carnations, poppies or cornflowers–and what about royal-blue satin pansies?

Use your imagination and experiment with fabric samples or offcuts.

Do not forget leaves create an added touch of realism; try satin, glazed cotton, or velvet. To make blooms and leaves appear more realistic, fabric paint (such as Dylon) can be used to tint the edges or create subtle shading.

Before you start to experiment with flower making, make sure that you have adequate references on which to base your designs. It is easy to fool yourself that you know exactly how certain flowers look, but it is better for that extra touch of realism, to have good references to copy. If you cannot obtain real flowers for this, use a gardening book or an illustrated calendar.

It must not be forgotten that some artificial flowers are not meant to look real, but are merely an extension to a costume. If possible, use offcuts of the costume fabric for such decorations, which can then be added to a contrasting hat, or pinned on to a lapel to create an *haute couture* effect. Special care should be taken when using fabric flowers to brighten an otherwise drab costume; try to link the colour with the scenery or props on the set, or maybe another costume. Always consider each detail as a part of the whole set which the audience sees.

The main principle of moulding artificial flowers is that fabric petals can be shaped by using a heated curved implement. Professional flower makers have a special tool, much like a metal ball on a stalk which is set in a wooden handle. The ball is heated and pressed on to the petal shapes which are resting on a sawdust-filled bag. You will be able to much the same thing by using an old spoon or melon scoop with a small firm cushion or an ironing pad underneath.

Camping gas or a gas stove will provide a means of heating the spoon but do not forget to protect the hands with an oven glove. Test the heat of the spoon on scraps, then pass the back of the spoon on to the petal shapes until the required curve is achieved. (The crinkled edge will be dealt with later.)

Basic flower shapes

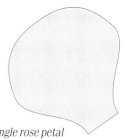

Single rose petal

Tiny blossom

Moulded rose

Carnation

Here are a few simple outlines which you can copy and use as templates, but do experiment with your own shapes too.

For all the flowers You will need

A card template
Pencil
Small, sharp scissors
Small firm cushion, or an ironing pad
Latex adhesive
Florist's wire
Florist's green binding tape
Spray starch

To make a rose

You will need the previous items plus a metal knitting needle. Use plain scissors for the rose shapes.

Stage 1

Trace off six copies of the tri-petalled shape, cutting these shapes from the fabric with sharp scissors. (Try to avoid a ragged edge.)

1 Mould the petals, pressing a hot spoon on to the cut shapes so that the petals curve inwards and have a tendency to overlap.

2 Select the first set of petals, overlapping them and gluing into place. Thread this on to the florist's wire which has been looped at the top. Glue base with each layer.

---

3 Pleat the base, securing with adhesive to create a bud-like shape.

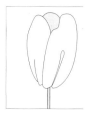

4 Repeat this process (apart from the pleating) with each layer, making the overlap less and less each time.

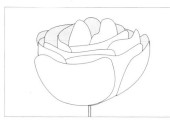

5 Carefully place each layer on to the florist's wire so that each petal join is overlapped by a complete petal.

Stage 2

6 Allow the adhesive to dry, then spray the whole flower with spray starch, keeping the petals away from any other surfaces which might distort their shape or stain them. (Placing the flower in a vase first is possibly the best way for this.)

7 Heat up the needle end and use this to gently prise apart the petals. Roll the petals outwards over the needle to give the characteristic contours of rose petals.

ou will find that the heated needle will also iron out any crinkles at the outer edges of the petals.

3 Once you are satisfied with the overall shape of the rose, bind up he stem with green florist's tape, uilding up the layers just beneath the etals. If you wish to achieve greater ealism, paint the edges of the petals vith fabric dye–one shade darker than hat of the fabric.

Note As an alternative, assemble the ose in a similar way, but this time cut-ing out individual rose petals. The esult is possibly more realistic as the etals are varied in shape. However, it s more time-consuming because the ase of each petal has to be bound with orist's wire in order to secure the etals into position.

For other flowers: try using pinking hears to create a ragged edge, or cut ircles of fabric radially for a fuller oom-pom effect. Ease the layers apart fter starching. (No heating will be re-uired for these.)

To make a carnation

A circle just a little larger than three nches (7.5 cms) in diameter is suit-ble for a carnation. Cut perimeter vith pinking shears, then make three adial slits almost to the central hole.)therwise follow the basic instruc-ions for making a rose.

Flower sprays

The best way to display similar flowers is in a spray. Artificial bead stamens can be purchased from craft shops, al-though it is often more satisfying to make even these from odds and ends around the home. Corks, small buttons (pearl ones are ideal), beads, small shells, circles of textured fabric, and even dried seed heads can be threaded or glued in the centre of the flowers.

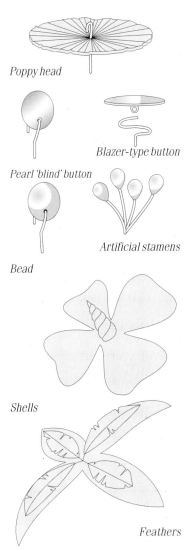

Poppy head

Blazer-type button

Pearl 'blind' button

Artificial stamens

Bead

Shells

Feathers

Leaves from fabric

A simple fast way of making leaves suitable to add to artificial flowers uses iron-on hemming tape which has adhe-sive on both sides.

Hair ribbon (especially velvet) is very good for this purpose as it has an at-tractive surface and can be bought in varying widths to suit the leaves re-quired so there will be little waste. However, any fabric, in fact, will do.

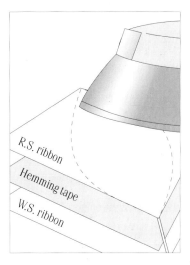

R.S. ribbon

Hemming tape

W.S. ribbon

Set the iron according to the tempera-ture suggested on the hemming-tape pack. Press the layers of ribbon, tape, and wire until sufficiently bonded. Cut the leaf to the required shape, if neces-sary binding the stalk with green florist's tape. Darken the edges of the leaf, and paint in the veins with fabric dye for more realism.

Another interesting way of developing this process is to use the actual leaf shapes that appear on printed floral material. Of course the underside will have to be plain so make sure it is of a matching colour. Careful positioning of the wire to correspond with the central vein of the printed leaf is, of course, es-sential to complete the effect.

Appliqué leaves

An effective extension to this second method of making fabric leaves is to use this process in conjunction with appliqué. This kind of assemblage creates a garment which may well fall in to the 'for keeps' category, as the process is quite time-consuming. However the end result will justify the extra effort. For this reason it is worth considering for a special dress.

The scope of these skills need not to be limited merely to flowers and leaves.

You will need

Fabric (which links up design or colour-wise with the rest of outfit)

Iron-on Vilene (or a similar iron-on interlining)

Scissors

Sewing materials

Milliner's wire
(instead of florist's wire)

Iron-on hemming tape

The same techniques can be used to extend into three dimensions and can create many designs, such as butterflies, a flower fairy or swirly dramatic shapes for a 'sci-fi' conqueror from outer space–or perhaps just to lift an otherwise drab jacket, using geometric shapes as found in the early sixties.

1 Bond a section of fabric to the interlining, setting the iron in accordance with the instructions on the interlining pack.

2 Decide which prominent parts of the design you wish to apply to the costume–a group of flowers, for instance. Cut this out, then tack (baste) it into position.

3 Using a close zig-zag machine stitch, sew the edges of the appliqué into position. The thread can be matching or contrasting.

4 Select leaves from the design on the remaining fabric (or use some ribbon) and follow the leaf-making instructions on page 69. Use a coordinating or contrasting fabric for the underside of the leaf and, if desired, zig-zag over the leaf edges, taking care to avoid the wire stems.

5 Oversew the leaves to the appliqué, catching the top and bottom of each leaf (or wherever seems appropriate). Additional decoration can be hand sewn–maybe beads or sequins and embroidery thread could be sewn on too, helping to emphasise line, colour, or texture.

Flowers from feathers

Many exotic flowers can be made from feathers–which, after all, are not dissimilar to petal shapes. Feathers are reasonably resilient as a costume accessory and will 'bounce' back to shape if ruffled.

Finding a good supply can be a problem. Go to a local specialist meat supplier where you may acquire chicken, turkey, goose, pheasant or even partridge feathers, with possibly some more exotic plumage from other birds. It will probably prove too expensive to purchase feathers from a craft shop unless only a very small quantity is required but you may be able to collect your own.

Feathers with strong markings make a wonderful contrast to those which have been dyed.

To dye

Use a hot-water dye; submerge the feathers completely for at least one minute, constantly moving them to facilitate even dyeing.

A helpful hint: Add small lengths of fabric collars or cuffs to this dye bath. They may come in useful as costume trimmings and will colour co-ordinate with the feathers.

Trimming feathers to shape

Hold the edge to be cut quite closely to ensure that the cut is even, not ragged. Use sharp scissors. Haircutting shears are ideal, as one long cut along the edge is far better than tentative, broken trimming.

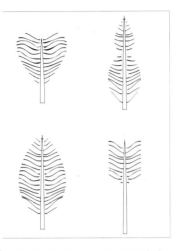

Feathers can be pulled and curled to break away from their predictable shape. Curl them in much the same way as paper, dragging a ruler, knife or the blunt edge of the scissors along the quill, right to the tip of the feather. Then it will spring into a curl. ◇

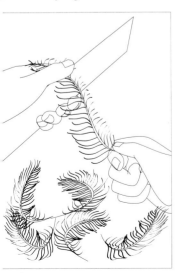

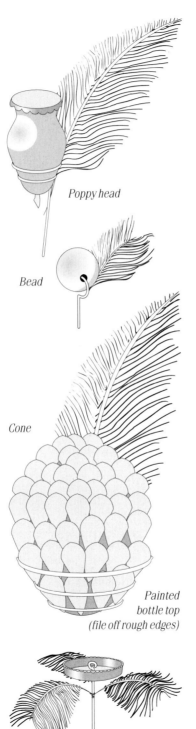

Poppy head

Bead

Cone

Painted bottle top (file off rough edges)

Assemble feathers, binding them with wire around a stem of florist's wire, to which has been threaded, wired, or glued an artificial stamen.

Use an assortment of artificial centres or stamens.

The radiating design of petals is not always appropriate. Do not be frightened of extending the 'petals' on one side to create a different asymmetrical shape.

Remember that some feathers, notably dark brown or golden yellow, can be used to imitate autumn leaves: their shine is reminiscent of the gleam on beech leaves.

Making artificial feathers from stiffened fabric or paper

Animal costumes

There are basically two kinds of animal costume: the upright 'humanoid' animal–when often it is mainly the head, mask or make-up which conveys the animal's identity, and the 'on-all-fours' animal–when the entire animal is likely to be dressed.

The costume approach might aim at realism or be an interpretative image.

Masks and head-dresses are often a vital part of the costume and the many different ways of making these are dealt with in detail in the next chapter.

Whether a humanoid, realistic or fantastic approach is used, the first task is to analyse the basic 'ingredients of the particular animal character and, armed with this information, create costumes which help the actor to convey this character through costume.

For the 'humanoid' interpretation, a leotard and tights can form a basis for many costumes and accumulating a good collection of these will be very useful. Dance and ballet schools frequently enact animal roles and may be a good source of costumes to borrow–or, at the very least, a source of ideas and inspiration!

Analysing the animal ingredients

Take a trip to the library to look at as many images of the animal as possible; watch any television documentaries or films featuring the particular creature and any other productions when animals are enacted. If there is an opportunity to watch the animal in real life, this is the greatest help of all.

With domestic pets such as cats and dogs, studying form is fairly straight-forward, although dogs do cover a vast range of shapes, sizes and colour so it will be necessary to select a breed first. Other animals may involve a trio to a pet shop, zoo or farm–observation of insects in the back garden or wildlife in the fields and woods! Make notes and drawings and build up a dossier which will be helpful for future productions as well

Then talk to the director and actor to discuss specific character and interpretation of the role.

Physical attributes

It can be useful to examine soft toy patterns. Although these are of course on a much smaller scale they will provide lots of useful information on how to create the right shapes for heads, ears, paws and so on.

Physical attributes												
Animal	Face	Head	Body shape	Fur or skin	Eyes	Ears	Nose	Whiskers	Legs	Feet or paws	Claws	Tail
Shape												
Colour												
Texture												
Other details												
Movement												
Main 'natural' characteristics												
Theatre role												
Character												
Any special demands												
Complications												

Materials for animal bodies

Combined with a mask, head-dress or strong make-up, the animal body may be dressed in human clothing so as to suggest character. Alternatively the actor might wear simple trousers and top or a leotard and tights.

To complement the head or mask, the actor might wear human clothing in character with the animal role. This would suit many pantomime and fairy-tale characters such as those in *Toad of Toad Hall*, Beatrix Potter stories or some of the characters in *Alice in Wonderland*.

Sometimes it is sufficient simply to wear plain trousers and a top in black (or an appropriate main base colour). Or, perhaps, a bathing costume or a leotard and tights may be worn. If, however, the animal skin or fur has to be conveyed on the body as well as the head, there are many ways to do this—and you can be as imaginative as you like.

For example, some of the items in the following tables might be used:

Fabrics
Fur fabric
Old fur coats
Coats and capes
Towelling
Knitting
Wool or jersey fabrics
Felt
Velvet
Corduroy
Gabardine
Canvas
Hessian
Leather
Suede
PVC
Net

Rugs and bedding
Rugs - existing rugs can be used - sheepskin, cotton twist pile, striped Indian-style cotton rugs and hangings
Rug-making techniques to create specific colours and textures
Bedspreads Blankets

Once you have found a suitable fabric, it can be used to make head-dresses and/or sewn up into tunics, full body costumes, trousers, or dungarees.

Adapting a fabric base

Textures and colours may be painted onto a plain fabric, such as canvas or hessian. Do not attempt to paint fur fabric unless sprayed through a stencil or it will clog.

Patches, rags, raffia, string, wool, card, foil, beads, sequins, old tights, paper, material strips, scales, or feathers might be sewn onto a suitable base

The animal body might be suggested by a simple loose-flowing tunic or the fabric can be built on to a frame to create a three-dimensional shape.

Wings

Galvanised wire can be bent into shape and then bound together with fuse wire or strong carpet thread. Net, muslin, organdie or plastic cling wrap can be used for the wing material which can be sewn into position or glued onto the wire frame–and then, if required, decorated with feathers, metallic spray paint, foil shapes, sequins and so on.

Feathers can be made from paper or fabric. If they are given a wire 'stem' they can be usefully bent and adjusted. See also page 71.

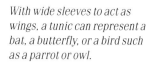

With wide sleeves to act as wings, a tunic can represent a bat, a butterfly, or a bird such as a parrot or owl.

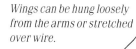

Wings can be hung loosely from the arms or stretched over wire.

By using a fur or woolly fabric or by adding suitable decoration–sew on or painted–a simple tunic base can represent all kinds of creatures, from a lamb to a ladybird .

Tails

There are all manner of tails from the cat's skinny pink or black version to the squirrel's fluffy extravaganza! The shape will depend on the animal concerned and some materials will suit short tails rather than long ones. The general style of costume is important too—if realism is intended, it is no use using glitter streamers! Anyway, here are some ideas:

Ways to make a tail

String and cord

Rope

Wool

Ordinary yarn, plaited, or knitted
Tassels, or pom-poms
(a fluffy pop-pom
is ideal for a rabbit)

A long round cylinder of fur fabric
or other suitable material
can be various widths and might
hang loose or be wired into shape

Stuffed stockings
or legs cut off tights
A feather boa

Net frill wound around a wire frame

Raffia

Sponge roll

Jointed sections of cardboard,
painted or covered and then linked
together on a cord
(for example, toilet-roll centres)

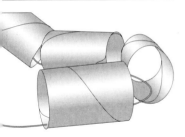

Ears

Ears might be an integral part of a mask or headpiece but if you do need to make them separately, here are a few basic shapes.

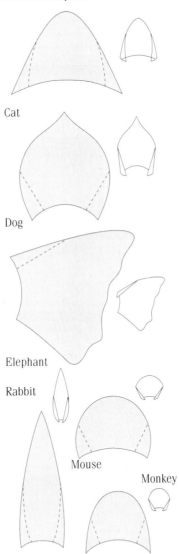

Cat

Dog

Elephant

Rabbit

Mouse

Monkey

String appendages

Antennae, claws and whiskers can be made from sized string that has been stiffened by dipping in glue. These may need to be reinforced with wire.

Costumes on cardboard, wire or hoop frames

Cylinders, cubes and cones can be made of cardboard and covered with fabric to create full size body sections. Lots of smaller shapes like this might be linked to create many-jointed arm and leg sections–good for insects.

A series of hoops can create a frame to make a long cylindrical body for a caterpillar, worm, snail or snake. With holes for legs, this might be used horizontally by several actors together or it could be allowed to trail behind a single actor.

For a vertical rounded frame, hoops or wire circles can be hung with fabric to cover an actor from head or neck to toe or knee. The fabric might hang below but make sure the last wire circle is above the knee so that the actor can move comfortably.

Similarly, when turning a single actor into an upright creature–whether, dragon, a crocodile or dinosaur–it may help to have a hoop or piece of cane to retain the rotundity of the animal body.

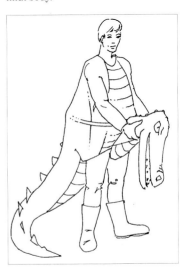

When more than two legs are required

Tableaux, pageants, comedy acts and pantomime will often require more than one actor to disappear into a single animal form. For example, two people are usually required for a horse, camel or cow while any number might lurk under the skin of a Chinese dragon.

1 Use chicken wire, basket reeds or steel wire to make a frame for the head, ensuring there are holes for the actor to see through.

2 Make the animal head out of the chosen material–perhaps fabric or papier mache and cover the wire structure. (Instructions for making papier mache and cloth mache) can be found in the section on creating shapes on page 45.

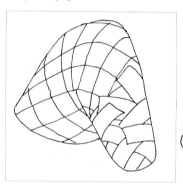

Paint basic colour if necessary.

Or

If the actor is to talk or sing a great deal, it may be preferable to make a head that wiill leave the face completely free.

3 Add any facial features still required such as eyes or mouth, painting on or sewing, depending on whether using papier maché or fabric.

4 A horse will need a mane and this can be made from wool or cord as shown below.

5 Make the animal body from fabric, sewing front and rear ends only and leaving a hole for the front actor's head at one end and a small one for a tail at the other.

6 Add any features–such as painting or patches–as required.

7 Attach tail and sew firmly in place.

8 Use tapes or a hoop to secure the animal body to the actors inside so that it will not fall off during any vigorous activity.

9 The actors will require suitable trousers or leggings to complement the costume.

A Chinese dragon can be made in a similar way but may hide a whole trail of people underneath.

ay attention to detail

ometimes the effect can be totally
uined if the make-up does not carry
ie costume theme on to the face.

ands and feet and any other extrem-
ies will need to be dressed suitably.
duck, for example, may benefit from
ebbed feet, made of felt over a ballet
hoe or slipper base and wired to hold
ieir shape. Also, socks can be pulled
ver the top of slippers or sneakers to
isguise these.

loves may need to be worn.–satin,
ool, lace or household rubber
nes–and claws may need to be at-
ached to these. Alternatively you
iay need to make paws.

oke shops have a whole host of ani-
ial masks and accessories and these
re certainly worth investigating.
ometimes it can be a good invest-
ient to buy the odd extra item rather
han to hire something. Moreover, the
urchase of one article might enable
ou to analyse the way it is made with
view to making your own version to
uit the particular need, if not this
ime–next time round!

Safety first

◇ Make sure the materials are not highly
inflammable (or that they are flame-
proofed) and that they are able to be properly
controlled by the actor–that he or she can get
up on the stage, climb any necessary steps
and that tall head-dresses or wide wings do
not hover close to any lighting equipment.

◇ Always make sure the actor can see
properly and that hoods and head-
dresses do not obscure vision. Moreover,
the actor's facial expressions may need
to be seen so check that any extravagant
head pieces do not obliterate the profile
in such cases.

◇ Make sure footwear
is secure–that it is
not likely to trip up the
actor or skid on a polished
stage flooring.

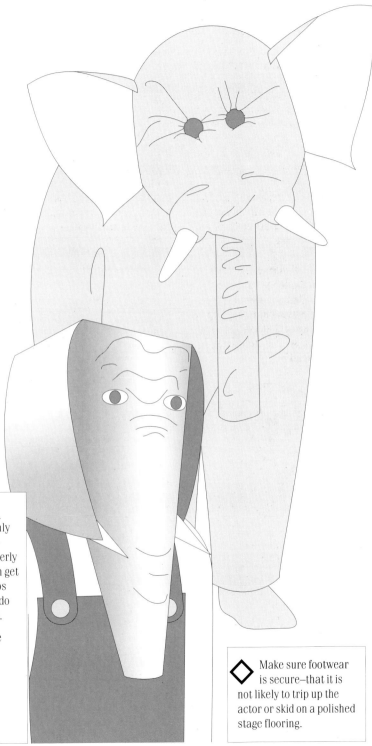

Masks

Masks were one of the earliest forms of theatrical costume, hence the comic and tragic masks from Greek theatre that are still used as an icon to symbolise drama.

The face is the most dominant part of the human form, with facial expressions conveying the whole range of human emotions. This means that a mask can be a very powerful way to suggest a different creature or character and masks are still used i dramatic, religious and festive cere monies in many different culture right around the world.

Types of mask

Giant carnival masks

Half-face masks

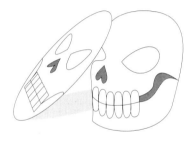

Masks can be flat or contoured.

Full head masks

Face masks

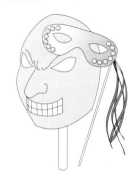

Masks held on a stick
(These might be flat, contoured, full-face, half-face or eye masks–flat ones can also be reversible.)

Eye masks

Closely related to masks are head-dresses when part of the face is actually seen. These might be full head masks but with some or all of the face area cut away.

There are also surround masks where the face is seen through a central cut-out–good for stars and flowers in children's shows.

Using masks

Masks are excellent when a dramatic effect is needed and marvellous for fast changes, transformations and for assuming a non-human role. They can eliminate a lot of time spent on make-up as even a small mask can completely change the appearance.

However, they are static and can be uncomfortable to wear for long periods. Even the briefest eye mask restricts vision, feels hot under the lights and is distracting if it begins to slip or to rub behind the ear lobes—so make sure that the mask is as good a fit and as comfortable as possible.

If the actor has to be audible it is important that there is plenty of space for the sound to come out. In general, half masks or open-faced head-dresses are better for a very busy actor with lots to say or sing.

Actors will also have to bear in mind that many masks are only effective when seen full face and this will effect the way they move.

Moreover, in a full mask, the real person's facial expressions are hidden and the actor has to learn to express emotions with hands and body language— this can take quite a lot of practice. If masks are to be used a good deal in a play, the wardrobe department will need to produce practice masks for rehearsals as soon as possible so that actors can become used to them and misleading gestures and body movements can be corrected before they become entrenched!

Masks are good for . . .

Animals, birds, fish and insects.

Fantasy creatures—vampires, robots, aliens, dragons, monsters, sprites, fairies, elves, demons and nursery rhyme characters such as Humpty Dumpty or The Man in the Moon.

Extreme human caricatures—such as pirates and gypsies, clowns, witches and witch doctors, ghosts and skulls—especially if there is insufficient time to alter make-up.

Non-human forms that have come to life—such as fruit, cakes and other food, flowers and trees, Aladdin's lamp, sun, stars and moon.

Abstract ideas and emotions such as the elements (fire, earth, water), happiness and sorrow, Fate and Death.

Materials

Anything goes! Much depends on the style of the production, of course, and masks can be anything from a plain black eye mask to a tiger's face, an elegant creation for a seventeenth-century masqued ball, a stocking pulled over the head or a bird's plumed extravaganza, flourishing glimmering feathers. Anything mentioned in the jewellery section on page 64 might also be considered. Be adventurous, experiment!

Lightly-boiled eggs can be scooped out and the shells painted with PVA glue and paint to make prominent eyes or rounded nose (see page 153).

The tops of plastic containers can be cut into interesting shapes. The handle will make a useful nose.

Anything mentioned in the jewellery section on page 64 might also be considered.

Consider using the following and combining different materials

Fabric
Fabric on card
Stockings
Paper
Card and cardboard
Corrugated card
Paper bags
Wood
Willow caning
Calico stretched over cane
Cheesecloth
String
Straw
Metal foil
Boxes
Large plastic containers
(the kind that holds
milk or juice)
Tissue on card
Fur fabric
Feathers
Papier maché
Paper plates
Foam rubber
Liquid latex

The features and other details on a mask can be painted directly on to the mask or made from all sorts of household items or craft materials, including

Plasticine or Fimo
Felt
Clay
Sequins
Buttons
Bottle tops
Egg boxes
Wire
Card

Hair

Eye masks

Page 78 shows a basic eye mask. This simplest of all masks can be extended and added to in all sorts of ways to make a huge variety of masks– so it can range from the simple black eye covering for a robber to exotic bird faces with colourful beaks and crests of feathers–or a cat–or a butterfly.

Paper bag and box masks

These are simply bags or boxes painted to depict a face or animal, with any necessary appendages attached. They can represent almost anything from an octopus with dangling tentacles, to a robot or a king.

A cardboard mask

Many face and animal masks can be bought ready made but it is fun to experiment with making your own.

Human face masks are generally flat , curving when the elastic goes around the head. Animal masks, however, look more convincing if three-dimensional with a beak, snout or muzzle– and ears that curl appropriately.

Basic human face shape

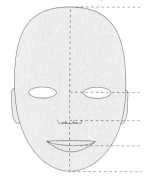

A mask made from a corner of a cardboard box.

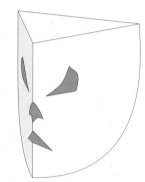

Mask made from a paper plate.

Papier maché or cloth maché

Papier maché or cloth maché (a cheesecloth and thinned glue mix is good for this purpose) can be built up on a clay form, onto a shape cut from a strong cardboard box, or over a balloon or a wire frame.

balloon-based mask

You will need

One balloon
Paper
(brown paper, newspaper,
paper towels, tissue)
Wallpaper paste
Water
Shellac
Bucket

*If you prefer, you can use cloth
and carpenter's glue instead of
paper and paste.*

Optional

Balloons or plastic tops or cups
for features

1 Inflate the balloon to the required size and then stand it on a cardboard collar to hold it secure while you work.

2 Securely tape in place anything being used to make ear or nose shapes (for example, other small balloons, polystyrene cups, plastic tops, or shaped clay).

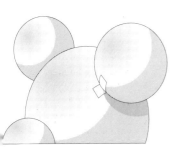

3 Coat the whole balloon surface with petroleum jelly. Then cover with papier maché strips. Build up several layers using paint in the mix in alternate layers as described on page 45.

4 Leave to dry. Let out the air when the papier maché has set.

5 If necessary, trim away any excess material to fit.

A balloon based mask may be used as a solid head. Alternatively, it might be sliced in half and used to create two face masks.

Instead of papier maché, a balloon can be surrounded with a criss-cross network of string that has been dipped in carpenter's glue.

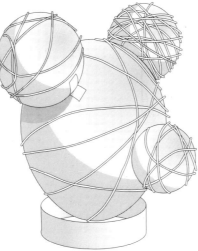

This string and glue method can also be used to create crowns and head-dresses. Once the basic network has been established, the final surface layer can be designed to use the string in interesting patterns.

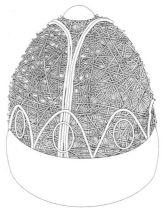

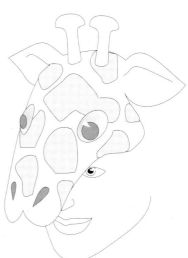

A mask might be made to sit on top of an actor's head to allow him or her to see and speak clearly if the role demands this.

The mask can be made of papier maché or any of the materials already described. Foam rubber is useful because it is light and will not be top heavy.

Making a mould

Masks can also be constructed on top of a mould.

These moulds might be made of clay, or plaster and sandcast, or created directly over the actor's face so that the fit is excellent. You can use dental moulage applied over the actor's face which sets into a rubbery material and reproduces minute details.

You will need
Straw and cotton wool
Swimming cap
Alginate
Bandage impregnated
with plaster
Dental plaster
Water

1 Cover the actor's hair with a swimming cap and the facial hair (including eyelashes) with gauze stuck down with petroleum jelly. Make sure the air spaces–mouth and nostrils–are kept clear by first plugging the nostrils with cotton wool or straws and inserting a straw in the mouth. Tell the actor to stay very still and to keep the eyes closed.

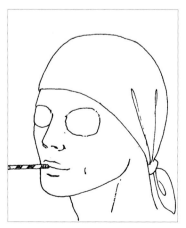

2 Mix and melt and then apply the alginate moulage, working fairly quickly as it sets fast. Mix small quantities at a time. The colder the water, the slower the alginate sets.

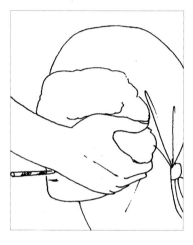

3 When the alginate is dry, build up a good layer of strips of plaster cast bandage–or your own mix of plaster and scrim–over the alginate.

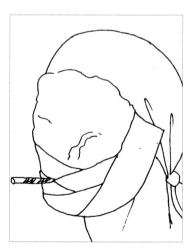

4 Remove the mould a few minutes later, once the plaster has dried.

5 Mix up some dental plaster and fill the negative mould.

6 Once the plaster life mask is cool and set, remove it from the moulage (which can be used again, of course); leave to dry for 24 hours.

7 Paint the mould with shellac to protect the surface.

he mould could then, of course, be painted and used as a solid life mask but the reason for taking all this trouble is generally to create a mould around which other masks can be formed, the interior surface of which will then fit the actor perfectly. The new masks, whether of clay or papier maché, can be modelled with all sorts of new features like huge noses or bulging eyes.

Moulds like this can also be made with Flex Wax.

For a much quicker method, the actor's face can be covered with petroleum jelly, with tissue carefully covering any facial hair, and then two or three layers of small wet plaster bandage squares should be smoothed directly on to the actor's face to fit all the contours closely. This mould will set in about ten minutes and can then be used to create a positive cast in plaster of Paris.

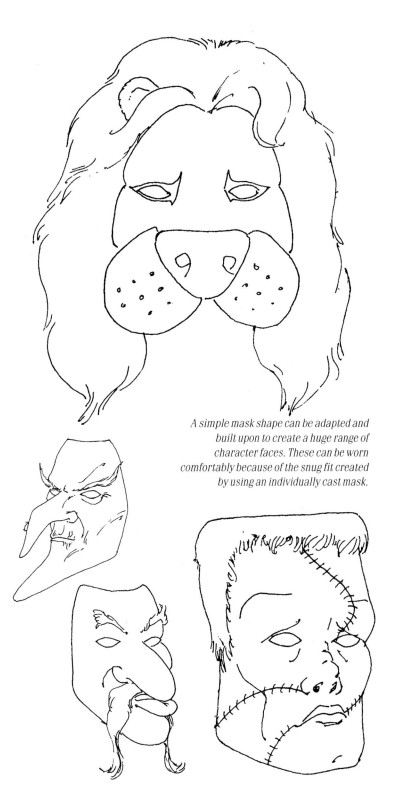

A simple mask shape can be adapted and built upon to create a huge range of character faces. These can be worn comfortably because of the snug fit created by using an individually cast mask.

Historical costumes

Making historical costumes

Once the actors don their costumes they begin to feel they are much more in character. With an historical costume this can be especially important as the performers step into another period of time—with all its accompanying manners and conventions.

For one thing, the actor will probably have to move differently, assuming the stately carriage demanded by a laced-up corset or crinoline or shuffling along in old cloth rags bound around the feet, manoevering in chain-mail and armour or swirling a villain's cape.

As well as helping the actor develop character, the audience are also greatly assisted in this transportation to another age when they see the dresses and styles that establish the historical setting.

To fulfil this, stage costumes need not be authentic in every tiny detail but they must convey the feeling of the period. One of the most important ways to achieve this is to capture the overall shape of the costumes, the way particular parts of the body were emphasised in different period styles to create a silhouette that will be unmistakably Egyptian or Elizabethan, Restoration or 1920s.

Research the period concerned as much as possible and analyse exactly what are the essential elements.

The basic costume shape may then be adapted to suit the overall style of the production and the particular characters too. And so, for example, shapes and colours may be exaggerated to suit a comic role while sweet soft colours and a high neckline will help to suggest a demure heroine.

Whatever the interpretation, the play will benefit greatly if the costumier has understood and then sympathetically conveyed the intrinsic style and atmosphere of the past.

The shape of the costumes alone can convey the historical setting of a play

Ancient Egypt

Plain bleached linen robes are draped over the body, sometimes worn loose and sometimes wrapped. All ranks from a servant to a prince might go bare-chested, wearing a loin skirt that finishes just above the knee. Those of the dignitaries, however, should be decorated by a fine decorative girdle.

The chief distinguishing features which denote 'Egypt' are the rich circular collars, originally made of bands of metal and stones and the angular styled and braided wigs, with pointed beards for men in authority and distinct eye make-up for all.

A loin cloth can be a simple piece of fabric draped and tied around the body but this takes time and if it is not done properly can leave the actor feeling a little insecure so it is probably better to cheat and stitch appropriately draped fabric onto an elastic waistband or a belt or onto underwear or bathing briefs.

The linen robe (or kalasiris), which is suitable for a male or female, can be made from a simple very wide tunic, as shown overleaf.

Suggested fabrics

Cotton sheets can provide an economic source of white fabric, especially old ones of course.

Cheesecloth or butter muslin will drape well and are not too bulky when gathering into folds.

Wool crepe and jersey are expensive but will give a good effect for the more regal garments.

A prince, priest, guard and servant: all might wear a loin skirt (or shenti).

Making the kalasiris

1 Cut out one front and one back. The bottom edges can be curved or straight.

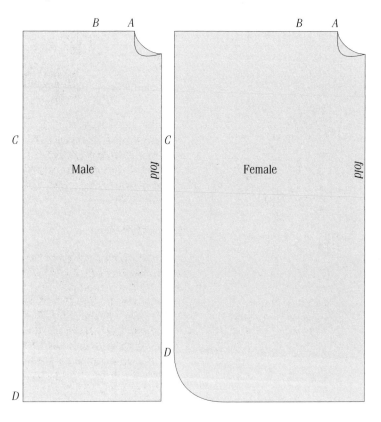

2 Join the shoulder seams, leaving a gap on one side from A to B to ensure neckline is large enough to go over the head. Clip edge of neckline so the curve is 'relaxed' and then turn in and stitch neckline.

3 Make a fastening at neckline (see page 36). There is no need to worry about authenticity: choose whichever method you prefer as the neckline will be hidden by the collar.

4 Join side seams from C to D and then turn in and hem all the remaining unstitched edges.

5 Cut out a sash. This might be fairly narrow and made in a plain matching fabric–or a wider sash in a rich contrasting material if the wearer is of some eminence.

6 Sew edges of sash, leaving a gap for turning and then turn right side out. Press and then stitch up opening.

7 The kalasiris can be draped and tied in many ways. It might be simply gathered in with the sash or, for a woman, clasped by a brooch to gather in the sleeve folds, and then tied with a sash. A woman might wear a simple narrow sheath gown either with short sleeves or with wide shoulder straps to leave the arms free for working. This might be worn alone or underneath the kalasiris.

Accessories

Shoes

Depending on how many splinters lurk in your stage flooring, the actors should either go barefoot or wear simple sandals.

Jewellery

The aristocracy made much use of fine jewellery and gold and enamel ornament. Necklaces, spiral earrings, bangles and arm bands worn at the wrist and above the elbow will help to give the right effect.

An Egyptian necklace or collar

You will need

Felt
Decorative bits and pieces such as beads, bottletops and pasta
PVA (white flexible) glue
Paint

Beads can be made with papier maché or Fimo. These can be painted or sprayed and then threaded together to make a necklace–or used to decorate a circular collar.

1 Cut out a circular collar from the felt.

2 Sew hooks and eyes on the two open ends.

3 Decorate collar by gluing on beads, tesserae, nuts, bolts, pasta, felt pen tops, bottle tops–or whatever might look appropriate camouflaged with PVA (white flexible glue) and then painted.

Head-dresses

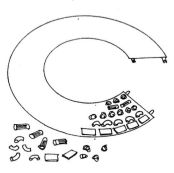

These might be made from fairly stiff material, usually horizontally striped in blue and white, cut and draped as shown above.

A helmet with a snake feature can be built from papier maché over a balloon with a ping-pong ball on the top. The cobra is made from cardboard reinforced with wire.

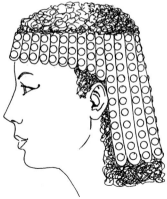

A Nefertiti type head-dress can be made from cardboard or stiffened fabric, rolled into a cone and then, if necessary, trimmed to final shape as shown.

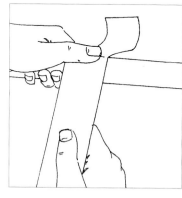

A curled tail should be added at the back. This might be made from card wired into shape or from drawing paper curled by pulling a strip tightly over the back of a ruler, from one end to the other.

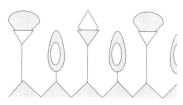

A head-dress can be made of medallions (bottle tops or buttons covered or sprayed gold) glued or sewn onto lengths of tape or ribbon and attached to a wire circle or elasticated band.

Finishing touches

It is useful to find pictorial references of Egyptian artefacts and decorative work. Study their symbols and hiero-glyphs and then try to use the kind of patterns they implemented. Motifs were generally taken from the natural world around them–plants and flowers like the papyrus and lotus, feathers and birds like the owl and vulture, and many other creatures such as snakes and the scarab beetle.

Egyptian motifs

Stencils can be used for repeating patterns. If realism is intended, colours should be restricted to those produced by the simple vegetable dyes then used–such as the rusty reds and strong blues produced by indigo and henna.

Ancient Greece

Ancient Greeks wore simple linen, wool or cotton chitons or himations.

Basically, a chiton is a length of material wrapped around the body and then pinned at the shoulders and tied at the waist. Men wear a short chiton and women a longer version. By using belts or cords around the waist and criss-crossing the breasts, the chiton can take on a wide variety of shapes and styles that often resemble separate skirts and blouses—so much so that the costume might be created as two separate pieces should large pieces of fabric be in short supply.

The himation is a rectangular length of fabric about twelve to eighteen feet long (about 4-6 metres) that can be draped in many different ways but which is usually worn so as to leave the right arm free. It might be worn instead of, or together with, the chiton.

Suggested fabrics

As with the Egyptian garments, softer fabrics are especially suitable for the more diaphanous women's costumes while lightweight cottons and woollen fabrics are good for men's lengths. If fabrics are draped and pinned or loosely stitched, rather than cut, they may be very useful, rearranged into other costumes in future productions.

Cotton sheets are good for making the chiton but you will several joined together to make a full-length himation.

Cheesecloth or butter muslin drape well and are not too bulky gathered in folds or bunched at the shoulders.

Towelling is good if it is not too coarse.

Wool crepe and jersey—these are expensive but good for the more sophisticated garments.

The chiton

A male chiton would be cut from fabric as shown here or cut to a longer length if for a woman. For a woman, the longer Doric chiton has an extra fold at the top to create a draped 'cape' effect.

armhole   neckline   armhole

Pin front and back together at shoulders

seam

fold or seam

Short Chiton

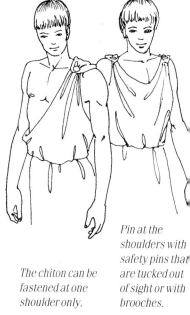

The chiton can be fastened at one shoulder only.

Pin at the shoulders with safety pins that are tucked out of sight or with brooches.

A fold or overlay at the top might be angled or cut to create various interesting effects.

If the fold is deeper, when the chiton is gathered in at the waist this extra fabric creates a pleasing skirt overlay.

A wider chiton can be pinned at intervals or gathered and sewn to create sleeves.

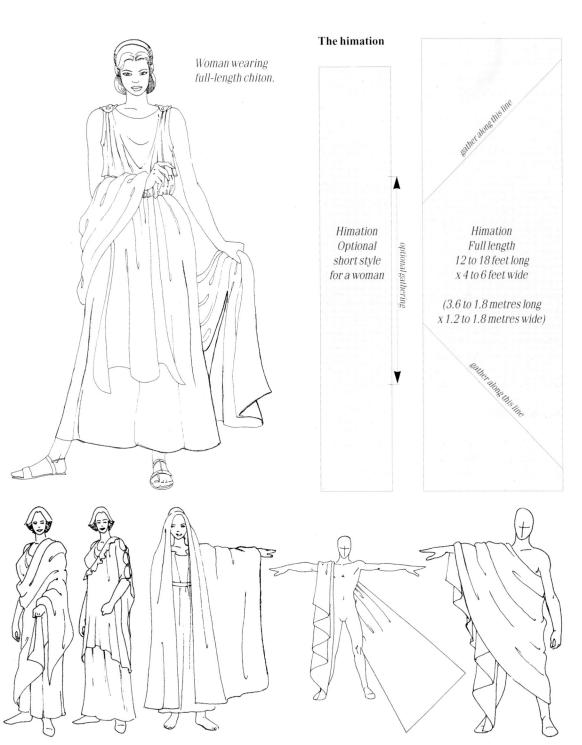

Woman wearing
full-length chiton.

The himation

*Himation
Optional
short style
for a woman*

optional gathering

gather along this line

*Himation
Full length
12 to 18 feet long
x 4 to 6 feet wide*

*(3.6 to 1.8 metres long
x 1.2 to 1.8 metres wide)*

gather along this line

For a woman, the himation can be long, or
short, or draped to cover the head.

The long length of fabric can be gathered first along the two diagonals as
shown so that it falls more naturally into folds from the shoulder and arm.

Accessories

Feet might be bare or simple leather or rope sandals can be worn, or, for men, thonged sandals with the thongs continuing up to beneath the knee.

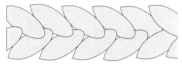

Head garlands can be made by cutting out leaves from felt with a central vein of wire so that their angle can be adjusted and then sewing these leaves onto a piece of tape or an 'Alice' band or elasticated hairband.

Finishing touches

Reddish brown dyes were very popular. Strong geometric borders–like those used on the ceramic decoration of the time–add a convincing touch.

Armour

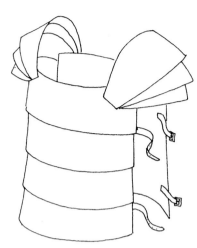

> #### For the armour, you will need
>
> *Felt or carpet underfelt*
> *Blanket material stiffened with shellac*
> *or*
> *Mock leather (see page 43)*
> *Glue*
> *Paper fasteners*
> *Rope or cord*
> *Aluminium*
> *Nuts and bolts*
> *Metal tabs*
> *Old belts*
> *Corrugated card*
> *Ties or elastic*
> *Stapler and staples*
> *Wire snippers*

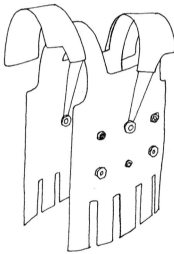

Breast armour can be made of mock leather (see page 43) or thick felt or carpet underfelt or old blankets stiffened with shellac.

> #### To make a helmet you will need
>
> A wire frame or a balloon
> Papier maché ingredients
> (see page 45)
> Polystyrene, horsehair, card
> or drinking straws for the crest
> Glue

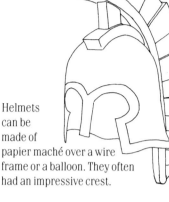

Helmets can be made of papier maché over a wire frame or a balloon. They often had an impressive crest.

Armour detailing:

Rows of felt scales, studs, nuts, bolts and washers, and tabs cut from aluminium (or pseudo metal tabs cast in plaster or made of Fimo) or will add the right heavyweight impression. Rivets can be made of glue drops or paper fasteners. Rope or cord can be sewn or glued around the edges and will look like a metal rim once it has been sprayed.

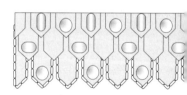

Greaves to protect the calves can be made from two layers of corrugated cardboard cut to shape and then stuck with their corrugated sides together together. They will need straps and/or elastic to keep them in place.

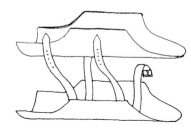

The Romans

The Romans drew much of their culture from Greek origins and so many of their clothing styles sprang from Greek counterparts but there are, in fact, quite a number of differences. One should be aware, of course, that the Empire covered a vast stretch of time and many different countries and some of the clothing mutated to absorb historic and climatic effects.

The most popular article of clothing was the tunic, made of wool or linen and worn at varying lengths by practically everyone in the Empire.

Gradually, dress became more extravagant as the Empire spread and, once Constantinople became the capital, trade with the East was established and cotton from India and silk from China arrived. Clothes became more colourful and, for the wealthy classes, were richly trimmed.

Suggested fabrics

For early Roman times, all the fabrics suggested for Egypt and Greece will be applicable but for the latter part of the Empire's rule, much more colour can be introduced so the range of fabric choice will become greater—and the opportunity for using old curtains will be increased!

The tunic

This is a simple garment and can be a 'standard' basic garment in the wardrobe to form the basis for all sorts of other historic garb—perhaps serfs, princes or biblical characters.

1 Fold fabric and cut out a shallow but wide neckline.

2 With right sides together, stitch up the side seams and then turn right side out and press.

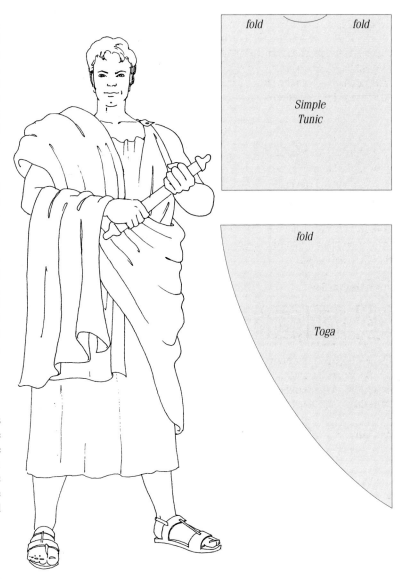

3 Finish the neckline with a narrow seam.

Made in a coarser fabric such as hessian or an old blanket and then tied with a rope this tunic will form the basis of a costume for a rustic Roman character and, in fact, for almost any man from the underprivileged classes—from Roman times to the end of the Middle Ages!

The toga

The toga was worn over the tunic and denoted official Roman citizenship. The toga of an official, such a magistrate, had purple bands.

The toga is made from a semicircular piece of fabric, and then draped over the shoulder rather like the Greek himation (see page 89).

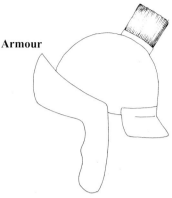

The stola and palla

For a woman, the palla, which was a large rectangular woollen garment, acted as the equivalent to the male toga. It was used a shawl and head covering.

The palla was worn over the stola, which was much the same as the Greek gathered chiton on page 88.

Accessories

Sandals were worn–lighter styles sufficed in Mediterranean areas but heavier-duty sandals were worn in the far northern reaches of the Empire–such as Britain.

Head garlands can be made as described for the Greeks on page 90.

Cloaks were often worn–over armour as well–and these were fixed in place with a large brooch.

Finishing touches

The Romans revelled in wearing jewellery and rings of gold, jet and other precious materials were worn on many fingers by both men and women.

By Byzantine times, rich embroidery was used on the clothing of privileged families.

Armour

Helmets are similar to Greek ones but are further back from the face with side pieces and visor-like fronts. They might be topped with the same kind of crests or with a circular crest of twine or hemp stiffened with shellac.

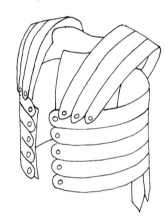

Breast armour can be made in similar ways to that described for the Greeks (see pages and 43 and 90). Breastplates were often built up in rows of circular bands and layers of metal scales hung below the waistline.

The stola is worn underneath the palla. The stola can be gathered or pinned at the top to create folds and sleeves. The palla is worn like a huge draped shawl.

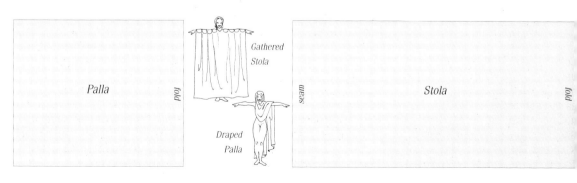

Palla

Gathered Stola

Draped Palla

Stola

Medieval times

Set the period with these simple basic shapes: long flowing gowns for ladies, and doublet and hose or knee-length (or full-length) tunics for men.

Costumes for the Middle Ages are useful for pantomimes, mystery and miracle plays, revues and musicals, as well as conventional plays with an historical setting. Also, many of Shakespeare's play are set in medieval and Tudor/ Elizabethan times. The medieval period covers a huge span of history but the basic body shapes of dresses and tunic or doublet and hose remain the same. It is the sleeve shapes, the necklines and trimmings and styles of hoods and hats that vary so much and add enormous interest–along with the addition of capes and surcoats.

To capture the essence of medieval times and immediately convey this to the audience, a simple bias-cut gown with fitted top, tight-fitting long sleeves, a wide curved or square neckline and a flowing fuller skirt suggests a 'Maid Marion' style. Or a dress with a close-fitting bodice, perhaps with a triangular insert, long wide hanging sleeves and a skirt that sweeps out from below the bust will suggest a 'Camelot' style.

Tunics or doublets and hose are the basic ingredients but there might also be soldiers in chain mail, ecclesiastical figures, knights in armour and peasants dressed in similar styles but made of rougher fabrics.

Suggested fabrics

The fall of the garment is all important for the ladies' dresses and men's capes and sleeves so use any fabrics which are relatively soft and yet heavy enough to drape well.

Ladies

Acrylics

Brushed rayon

Curtaining

Fine woollen and jersey fabrics

Linen

Gentlemen

Acrylics

Brushed rayon

Felt

Linen

Velvet

Woollen and jersey fabrics

Peasant characters

Dyed towelling

Old sheets and blankets, dyed if required

Hessian

Making a medieval dress

This dress can have a centre front seam that can be left plain or high-lighted in some way— for example with lots of small buttons, braid, embroi-dery or lacing.

The sleeves can be long and fitted or drop away as shown here and then worn over another dress, body, or sweater (with a low neckline or a polo neck)—with sleeves suitably trimmed.

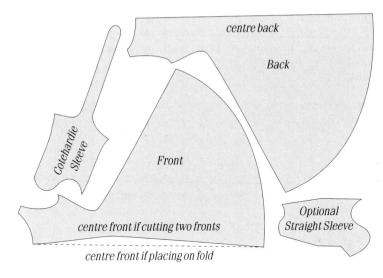

centre back

Back

Cotehardie Sleeve

Front

Optional Straight Sleeve

centre front if cutting two fronts

centre front if placing on fold

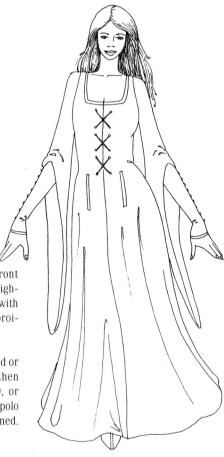

1 Cut out two back pieces, placing centre back away from the fold.

2 Cut out one front piece, placing the centre front line on a fold of fabric if you want a simple flowing front with no centre seam. *Or* cut out two front pieces, placing centre front on cut edges or away from the fold, if you want a centre seam that can be highlighted by embroidery or lacing.

3 Cut out two sleeve pieces—either two for the straight sleeve *or* two for the cotehardie flowing sleeve. (Ambitious sewers might combine both but the dress can be worn over a long-sleeved leotard!)

4 Join the two front pieces together, if not cut on fold.

5 Join the two back pieces, making a suitable fastening—either a hidden zip, Velcro or one of the other methods suggested on pages 36-7.

6 Join shoulder seams to attach front to back.

7 Gently gather top of sleeves to fit and then set into armholes.

Sew side seams of the sleeves and join the front and back sections together, stitching in one go from bottom of sleeve seam to bottom of skirt.

9 Finish neckline in one of the following ways.

Make a facing from bias-cut fabric, or clip curves and make a small hem, or turn under with bias binding, or finish edge and attach a decorative braid, cord or fur trim.

10 Hem bottom of skirt. Decorate seams and/or add lacing to bodice if desired.

11 Finish the cotehardie sleeve edges, perhaps trimming these with braid or fur.

Medieval sleeve shapes

Both dress and doublet can be altered to include any of the sleeve shapes shown for men and women.

Male version

Cut larger to fit male dimensions, and at a shorter length, this pattern will also serve to make a man's doublet.

For an Italian Renaissance figure or a courtier, a full-bodied shirt with full sleeves gathered at the cuffs can be worn under the doublet. If not worn over a shirt, a higher neckline might be needed. The fastening should be at the front rather than the back and accentuated with practical lacing or covered buttons and rouleau loops or frogging (see page 37).

A scalloped hemline will help give the right effect as suggested on page 96.

The doublet should be pulled in at the waistline with a belt and teamed with tights. Pointed shoes or small boots and, perhaps, a short cloak will complete the outfit.

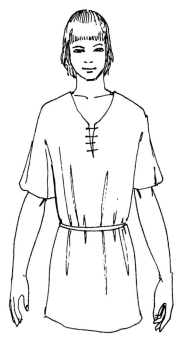

For a simple rustic tunic like this, see the pattern on page 91.

richer fabric. A variety of interesting hats will be fun to make and help enormously to set the period.

A simple bag hat can be made from a floppy bag (made from two arch-shaped pieces of fabric) and a stuffed circlet of fabric. The two bag sections should be joined together, turned right side out and then the bottom edge gathered to fit the stuffed circlet and sewn into place.

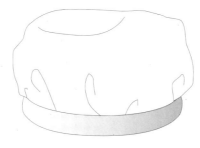

Shoes

Little pointed boots and pointed shoe were enormously popular. Shoes coul reach up to eighteen inches (46 cm) i length. (See page 62 for how to mak medieval pointed shoes.)

Bedroom slippers can be converte into medieval shoes for men an women. Thick woollen socks can b pulled over sneakers and rolled dow at the top.

Finishing touches

Men

Lots of stripes

Codpieces

Multicoloured tights

Men and women

Fur trimming

Lots of tiny buttons

Cord or fine rope belts (curtain cord)

Criss-cross lacing on bodices

Keyhole, castellated, zig-zagged or scalloped edges

Hats

Hats and head-dresses are a vital ingredient and include many fascinating shapes such as tall steeple-shaped hats, butterfly head-dresses and wimples. Men wore hooded capes, feathered caps in Robin Hood style or more flamboyant versions in

Hats and hoods

Different hood styles

The choice of hats is vast - mesh hairnets, hennins criss-crossed with braid, horned butterfly and wimple styles.

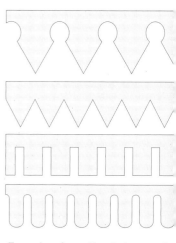

Examples of castellated, zig-zagged and scalloped edges.

Tudor and Elizabethan times

The Tudor period is still part of the medieval period in Europe but this section focuses on the kind of clothes worn in the sixteenth century, when the Tudors were ruling Britain and from when Elizabeth I came to the throne in 1558.

Fashion influences moved from Italy to France and Belgium. Then the clothes scene was dominated by Germany–garments were brightly coloured with many slashes to allow the material underneath to show. Finally, Spanish styles dominated, with stripes, stiff ruffs and collars and semi-circular capes, both short and long. The easy flowing garments of the early medieval period had gradually mutated into far more elaborate and formal shapes until by Elizabethan times, stiffened stomachers, padded hip pads and farthingales, ruffs or upright rigid collars and stuffed breeches had completely replaced the soft cascading lines.

Dressing the sixteenth-century man, from head to toe

Hat

It is easier to adapt an existing hat than to try and create a new one.

You will need

A brimmed hat

Circle of fabric
Plain, to colour co-ordinate with the hat's brim.

Thread
Colour matching

Feather
Or a wedge of 'fun-fur' or a tassel of fluffy wool which has been 'teased' out.

Sixteenth-century man

Hat

Ruff

Wings detail

Sleeve

Doublet (with optional peasecod belly)

Waist detail

Breeches (Venetian)

Garter

Hose

Shoes

A felt or linen hat is best. If you use straw, you will have to cover up exposed brim with fabric.

Dimensions: Measure up, across, and down the crown. Then add 6 inches (15cm) to this measurement, and this will be the diameter of the circle of fabric required, with ample allowance for the average crown. Before cutting out, however, it is a good idea to experiment first on scrap material, as crowns do vary and the particular shape and size of the hat concerned could require a slightly different area of fabric. (Extra fabric will obviously be needed if the brim is to be covered as well.)

Optional: If there is a marked colour discrepancy between the crown and the brim, use fabric paint to cover the whole of the hat.

To make the hat

1 Try the hat on the actor and trim away the surplus brim.

◆ Steam the brim, flattening or pulling it into shape whilst it is still damp. Allow the sides to gently slope upwards, with the front dipping down slightly.

2 Cut the circle of fabric according to the instructions above.

3 Pass running stitches along the circumference, allowing a half inch (15mm) seam allowance around the edge.

4 Place circle of fabric over the crown of the hat, and draw the thread, gathering the fabric to fit the headband. Oversew thread to fabric to fix the gathering as required.

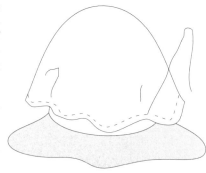

5 Using a finger (or the blunt end of scissors), push the raw gathered edge up under the taut thread.

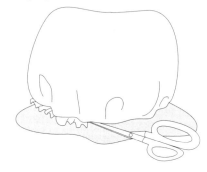

6 Oversew pouched edge, catching it here and there to the headband of the hat beneath.

7 Trim with a feather, sewing it into position and allowing the point to trail over the edge of the brim.

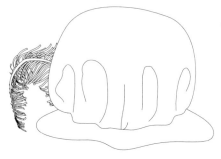

Doublet

If the actor is to have the characteristic peascod belly, you will need to make a padded undergarment before fitting on a doublet.

To make the peascod belly

You will need

An inner cushion

Thread

Half to one-inch (12 to 25 mm) wide elastic—enough to fit actor (measure with string).

Use a redundant cushion inner. (Foam filled is best as feathers tend to escape and tickle!) Otherwise, you can make up a cushion into the five-sided shape, as illustrated below.

1 Sew across the corner and then remove the shaded area.

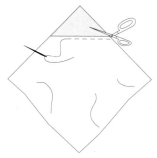

2 Sew elastic to the top seam, leaving enough spare to fit around the actor's shoulders and diagonally across the back.

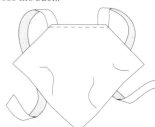

3 Sew ends of elastic on the two central corners.

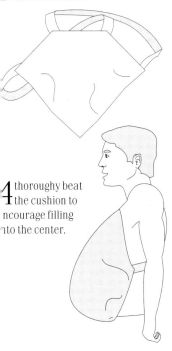

4 thoroughly beat the cushion to encourage filling into the center.

To make the doublet body

A plain-coloured 'jersey' type of fabric is suitable for this garment as it is stretchy enough to accommodate the simple curves of a sixteenth-century gentleman but not so stretchy as to become baggy. An oversized sweat shirt is ideal for this purpose.

1 Trim off the sleeves and cut a central line down the garment. Fold back an inch (3cms) seam allowance, and stitch the two hems by hand or machine, taking care not to stretch the fabric.

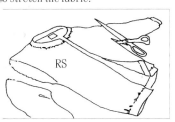

2 Turn the sweat shirt inside out and fit on to the actor (wearing a 'peascod belly', if required). Overlap and pin the front openings together.

3 Pinch and pin the fabric to create two parallel seams on either side (front and back). This will give the doublet the correct 'fitted' shape and attractive seaming detail.

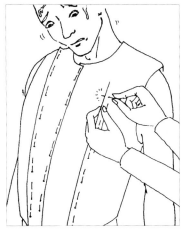

4 Trim away the surplus fabric on the lower edge, so that the front drops much lower than the back waist level to a central point.

5 Machine stitch the new seams, trimming off any bulkiness.

6 Stay stitch the lower hem, and encase or face the neck edge with self-coloured bias binding.

7 Turn doublet right side out. Sew on braid parallel to each side of the front opening and on either side of the two seams which go from the front to the back of the doublet. Instead of a braid, a colour-fast felt pen or fabric paint can be used to imitate braid. In this case, try to link up the colour with another part of the costume ensemble, perhaps echoing the feather or the garter colour. Braid can also be used for the buttonholes.

8 If preferred, use cord or make rouleau loops (see pages 36-7) to secure the front of the doublet. Sew on the appropriate buttons.

9 The padded waistband will need to be secured together at the back, to make a neat mitred point.

To make sleeves

It is quite simple to make a sleeve by following the pattern and measurement instructions on page 100.

Utilising the sleeves of an existing garment will be less time-consuming. Use cheap cotton or jersey. A striped fabric (such as pyjama material) will create an interesting contrast to the solid colour of the doublet. You will need a length of pre-gathered lace to trim the cuffs.

Making sleeves from pyjamas

1 Trim the sleeves away from the pyjama body.

2 Sew a lace 'cuff' to the bottom of the sleeves.

3 Sew new seams, tapering the sleeves. Carry on stitching over the lace.

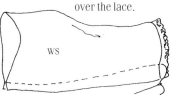

4 Trim off surplus fabric (and lace) at seam allowance.

Making a pattern and sleeve

1 Measure the actor's arm as illustrated below.

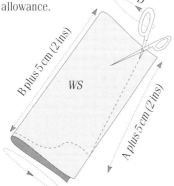

2 Fold a length of material along the straight of the grain. The width of the material need only be 6 inches (15cms) greater than the maximum circumference of the actor's arm (C). Pin along seam A and, whilst sleeve is still inside out, fit on to the actor, adjusting the seam allowance accordingly. Trim away any surplus seam allowance.

B plus 5 cm (2 ins)
WS
A plus 5 cm (2 ins)
D

C Plus 15 cm (6 ins)

3 Using this first sleevepiece as a pattern, cut the second sleeve.

4 Fold the lower edges of the sleeves to lower hems and stitch on pre-gathered lace along these edges. Sew seam A, extending seam across lace edges.

To fit the sleeve on to doublet

1 Turn the doublet inside out and slide the sleeve through the armhole so that the right sides are together and the lower armhole seams line up.

2 Pin this seam junction and evenly distribute the fullness of the sleeve 'shoulder' (giving preferential treatment to the back of the shoulder where more fullness is required). It may be helpful to place the pins as illustrated because then any gathers will be at right angles to the seam. This will also make tacking or basting unnecessary as a sewing machine will stitch straight over the pins.

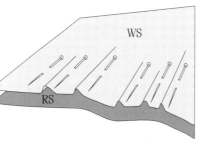

WS
RS

Do not worry about puckering or pleating of the sleeve top at the seam as the padded wings of the doublet will obscure any imperfections!

Wing and waist-roll detail

The outfit will look more attractive if the wings and waist roll can be made of the same fabric as the crown of the hat–to give the impression of a completely tailored outfit. Stretchy fabric would be particularly useful as both of these items are curved in all directions. If non-stretch fabric is used, it is advisable to cut the fabric on the cross to avoid too much creasing on the curves. Also, in this case, have a central seam at the back of the belt to avoid excessive wastage of fabric.

B   B
A

Measure the doublet body at A for the waist roll and at B for the wings (doubling this latter measurement). Add 2 inches (5 cms) to B and 4 inches (10 cms) to A for seam allowance and mitre adjustment. These measurements will enable you to gauge the length of both fabric strip and foam tubing required.

Waistband

1 Cut the foam length A and then cut it again transversely, as illustrated below.

A+10 cm (4ins)

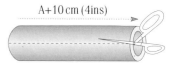

2 Mitre cut the ends to form a V which will match the V on the doublet front.

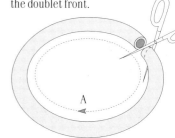

A

3 Cut out waistband fabric strip (joining two pieces at centre back necessary). Fold lengthways in alf, across ends. Create mitred dges. Cut at the same angle as the)am. Then stitch mitred ends.

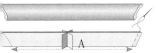

4 Turn right side out and insert foam, lining up the fabric and)am mitred points. Fold in seam llowances and overstitch edges. ttach waist roll to bottom of doublet.

Wings

1 Using measurement B as a guide, cut out the shape shown below (wice) in the fabric and cut lengths eeded from remaining foam. Trim off nds of foam to taper the shape.

2 With right sides together, sew the central portion of the seam as Illustrated. Turn the right side out nd insert foam or wadding, pulling nd prodding until the wing looks mooth and well rounded.

B+5 cm (2ins)

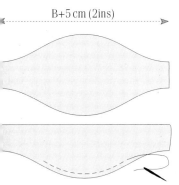

3 Invisibly hand sew the remainder of the seam, folding the raw edges inward and then oversewing them. Do not break off the surplus thread at the end as this can be used to anchor the ends of the wing on to the armhole seam of the doublet.

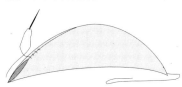

4 Fit the wings whilst the actor is wearing the doublet to check the positioning. It is better to set the wing slightly towards the back.

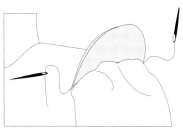

Breeches

An outsized pair of trousers can be utilised for this, although any sign of the twentieth century should bereremoved or sewn up (pockets, fly front, tabs, and so on). The waistband and seat area will have to be large enough to appear gathered and full on the actor.-

*Cut off waistband.
Dispose of tabs and/or buttons.*

Sew up fly opening

Remove zip

Sew up the pockets (reject any trousers with diagonally situated pockets) and remove inside and linings of pockets.

Remove any top stitching at fly opening.

Cut off surplus trouser leg.

Fold over waist band hem to take elastic; then stitch, leaving a small opening for access. Enclose one-inch (2.5 cms) wide elasticised waistband, using a safety pin to thread it through the casing hem.

Taper legs, checking lower leg measurement is large enough to take actor's foot, calf, and lower thigh! Hem bottom and thread narrow elastic through this.

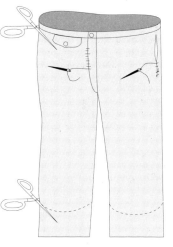

Garter

Although the garter may look casually tied in the decorative manner illustrated it is difficult to guarantee repeating this perfectly on successive occasions, and it is no easy matter to keep both garters identical. It is far better to assemble the looped tie and sew it on to the garter band, securing this with a snap fastener.

1 Fold over and sew together a length of fabric approximately 10 cm (4 ins) deep. Cut this length up to create the two garter bands, remembering to allow for an overlap.

2 Cut four shorter lengths for the looped bow decoration.

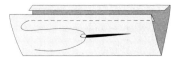

3 Fold bow pieces as illustrated. Gather centre up and overlap, sewing bow together at the centre.

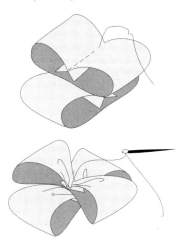

4 Sew bow on to garter, which is secured by snap fasteners. Attach garter on inside seam line of breeches hem, overstitching into place.

Ruff

There are no shortcuts to making this, and improvisation is most unlikely.

1 Measure neck and make inner collar to hold ruff. Use cambric, or a polyester cotton which has been stiffened with iron-on Vilene. Do not use coarse fabric or it will rub on the actor's neck.

2 Make a 'dog's collar', with extensions at the end which must be the same size as the depth of the ruff. Fix the inner ends together with two hooks and eyes, the outer edges with snap fasteners.

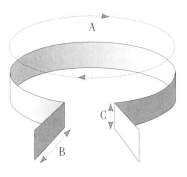

3 Cut a length of white fabric. Milliner's nylon 'crin' or nylon net is ideal as washing will not then be a difficulty. This is a very important consideration as it is most likely that the ruff will be smeared with make-up . This fabric will have to be about four times the outer diameter of the proposed ruff.

4 Fold the fabric as shown, making the fold width the same depth as the dog's collar.

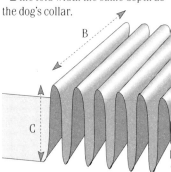

5 Hand sew top and bottom edges of the folds as illustrated, pulling the thread together so that it looks like this:

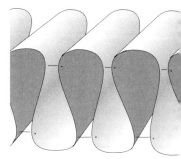

6 Attach the inner side of the ruff to the dog collar.

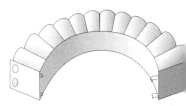

Elizabethan dress

Suggested fabrics

Stiffer fabrics can be used such as chintz and 'tapestry' type upholstery fabrics. Velvet ,velour , silk, corduroy and brocade are good but expensive so old curtains will do. They will make up to give an appropriately rich sumptuous finish.

Old evening dresses, if they are full enough, may provide fabric–if only for inset panels and sections.

> First you will need to construct the necessary undergarments
>
> A farthingale
>
> A hip roll or pads
>
> A boned corset

Farthingale

Use a child's hoop or cane, wire, a section cut from a plastic barrel, narrow flexible curtain rail or wire to make the farthingale hoop.

1 Encase the hoop in fabric. The top of the farthingale, the wheel, can be made up of two complete circles of fabric–or the circle can be constructed of several segments joined together.

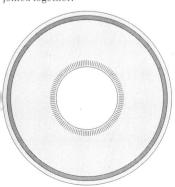

2 Run a drawstring or elastic through the waistline.

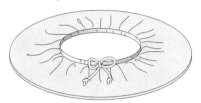

3 Cut a long length of material to make the skirt of the farthingale. This is attached to and suspended from the outer rim of the wheel.

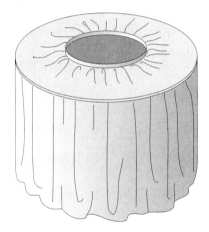

Hip pads and hip rolls

Hip pads or hip rolls can be stuffed with foam filing, kapok or chopped up tights and made in much the same way as the wings for the man's costume on page 101. They will then be attached to tape and tied around the waist to fit.

A hip pad

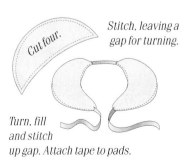

Cut four.

Stitch, leaving a gap for turning.

Turn, fill and stitch up gap. Attach tape to pads.

A hip roll

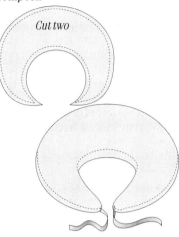

Cut two

Stitch, leaving a gap for turning.

Turn, fill and stitch up gap.

Attach tape ties.

The corset

Make up with heavy boning as described on page 44.

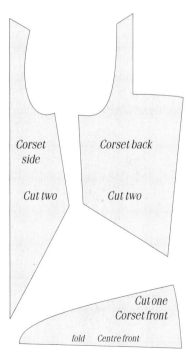

Corset side

Cut two

Corset back

Cut two

Cut one Corset front

fold   Centre front

The dress

This dress can be made up as a separate skirt and top to allow for greater versatility of sizing and future use.

The bodice

1 Cut out the bodice pattern pieces and sleeves. The pieces need not be in the same fabric. For example, the central front bodice section and cuffs could be in a contrasting fabric, or overlaid with lace.

2 Join the bodice sections together, leaving the centre back open.

3 Make up the sleeves and cuffs and then run gathering stitches along the shoulder edge, creating good strong gathers.

4 Set sleeves into bodice, adjusting gathers to fit, especially accentuating those towards the back of the shoulder, to give height.

5 Make back fastenings. Then the bottom edges should be finished neatly so that the bodice ends just below the natural waistline.

The collar

1 Cut out collar from either very stiff fabric or material that has been stiffened (see page 102).

2 Hem outer edge. Pleat or gather to fit neckline.

3 Add wire or stitches to control the pleating on the outer edge.

4 Attach to neckline. The collar suggested here is an upright 'fan' shape but a ruff can be substituted see page 102.

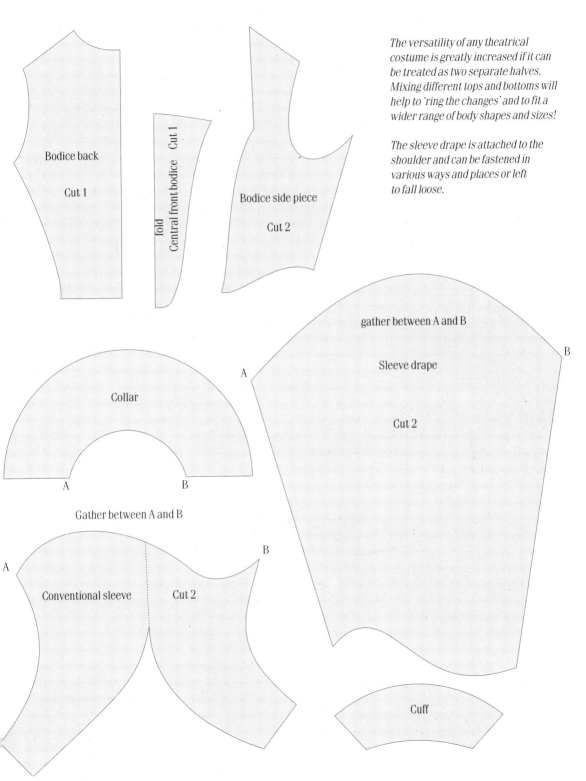

Bodice back

Cut 1

fold
Central front bodice Cut 1

Bodice side piece

Cut 2

The versatility of any theatrical costume is greatly increased if it can be treated as two separate halves. Mixing different tops and bottoms will help to 'ring the changes' and to fit a wider range of body shapes and sizes!

The sleeve drape is attached to the shoulder and can be fastened in various ways and places or left to fall loose.

Collar

A   B

Gather between A and B

gather between A and B

A

Sleeve drape

B

Cut 2

A

Conventional sleeve   Cut 2

B

Cuff

Skirt

Now make up the skirt. You will need a straight piece of fabric about 4yds (3.6m) long, preferably reversible.

1 Measure from waist to ground and mark line on fabric. Be sure you have allowed enough drop to take into account the farthingale and hip rolls which will be worn underneath.

2 Machine the Rufflette tape along the line you have marked.

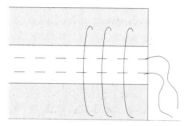

3 Turn over the top and bottom edges of the skirt and then join skirt back seam.

4 Pull up strings of Rufflette tape to fit waist measurement. The top section of material will fall over tape to create top frill.

5 Hem the skirt bottom edge as required.

If the material is not reversible, cut a separate flounce and join this to the skirt section (with the seam on the outside as this section will be reversed when the skirt is worn) before attaching the Rufflette tape.

The dress might be graced by the addition of hanging sleeves.

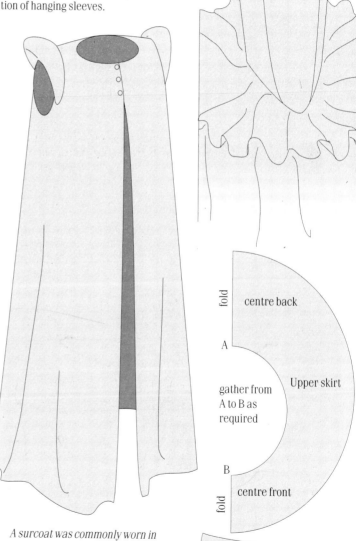

A surcoat was commonly worn in Elizabethan times. It might be sleeveless or with sleeves.

If you wish to make a stomacher you will need to elongate the front section on both the corset and the bodice, and will need to attach an upper skirt cut to the pattern shape shown, on to which a straight skirt piece can be attached.

fold

centre back

A

gather from A to B as required

Upper skirt

B

fold

centre front

Stomacher

centre front   fold

Accessories

Scented pomanders were suspended from the waistline.

Men wore garters—and medallions!

Men padded their paunches—and their breeches—using horsehair, rags or wool.

Shoes

Shoes had become very wide and square ended.

Heels did not appear until the end of the century.

Ruffs

Ruffs can be pleated, flared or open and upright.

Attach ruffs to ribbon which measures one inch (2.5 cms) greater than neck measurement and finish with Velcro, tapes, hooks or press studs. See also page 102.

Finishing touches

Men's clothes had lots of decorative slashes, opened out to show the fabric underneath—the fashion reached the point where outer garments were cut almost all over.

This can be suggested by cutting out fabric shapes and gluing on top of material—or fabric that does not fray easily can be folded and slashed—like paper lanterns!

Farthingales and padded hip pads and rolls are also very important. Without these foundation garments dresses

will not have the correct stature. See page 103 for further details on how to make these.

Quilting, overstitching soft fabrics and punching leather can create the right textured appearance.

By the time of the Spanish influence colours were more sombre.

Both bodices and skirts often had a central triangular panel in a contrasting fabric, richly trimmed.

Beads and aiguillettes were ornamental tags at the ends of cording, lacing and ribbon ties. They can be made from clay, Fimo, heavyweight aluminium foil or rolled paper or card. If time is short, tiny toggles will do—the sort used for bags and duffel-coats—the daintier the better.

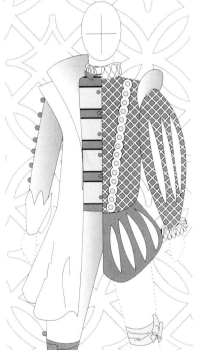

Slashing was a strong feature on men's clothing. There was also a good deal of topstitching, quilting, braiding and rows of tiny buttons.

The short breeches were slashed and padded.

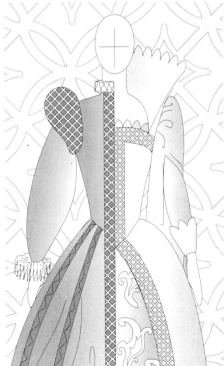

Women's dresses were decorated with quilting, beads, top-stitching, ribbon and braid.

Skirts and bodices often had central sections made in a strong contrasting fabric. Stencils and appliqué can be used to good effect on these.

Seventeenth century

This was a time of great extremes.

Extravagance in men's clothing became even more pronounced, with lace, frills and feathered hats in abundance. Think of the courts of Louis IV and Charles II, of curly black wigs and *The Three Musketeers* and the right images will spring to mind. This is the period that provides the setting for Restoration comedies and masques.

At the same time the Puritans were resisting such frivolity and their clothes echo the shapes but not the adornment—conjure up images of *The Crucible*, Oliver Cromwell and the Gunpowder Plot.

Men's 'suits' with matching jackets, waistcoats and breeches had arrived by the end of the century.

Suggested fabrics

Cotton: sheets and tablecloths provide a good source of white fabric, especially for collars and aprons.

Materials are much softer again— gone are the stiff brocades, and the stiff lines, of the previous century.

Satin and silks for ladies—lining material or old evening dresses may be an economic source.

Canvas, felt, leather and suede are excellent for men's waistcoats and breeches. Modern waistcoats and trousers can be doctored.

Making a man's costume

This basic costume can be left plain for a Puritan or trimmed lavishly with lace, flounces and bows to make a Cavalier version.

The shirt

The shirt can be an adaptation of an ordinary shirt, provided it is full enough and has generous sleeves.

Remove the modern cuffs.

The sleeves can be decorated with ribbons and elasticised at the wrist. (You may need to add extra fabric, having now removed the cuffs. This addition could be just a lace ruffle.)
or
You can make new cuffs.

Remove the modern collar and re-place with a new large square or pointed one.

The new collar and cuffs should be large and fluted–edged with lace for a Cavalier or left plain for a Puritan.

Breeches

These are worn longer than in the pre-vious century or were flared almost like a short skirt.

Once again, cut-down trousers or track-suit bottoms will suffice for the straighter versions–or a generous ladies' skirt or culottes might be doc-tored to create either gathered breeches or the skirt-like version.

The side seams and bottom edges should be lavishly trimmed for the Cavalier version.

Doublet or bolero

Make a sleeveless jacket or doublet. Once again an existing jacket or waistcoat can be doctored–seams slashed open up to the waist and trimmed with braid if appropriate.

Alternatively, a cropped 'bolero' style jacket with short flared sleeves can be worn.

Puritans often wore a more severe straight jacket with lots of buttons.

The cape

This should be long and plain for a Puritan–or short and lined with a flamboyant fabric for a cavalier.

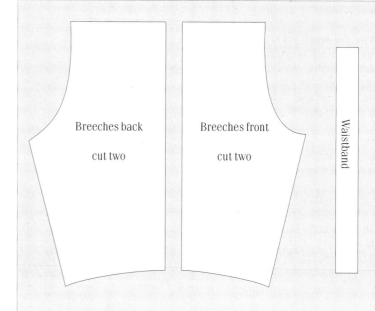

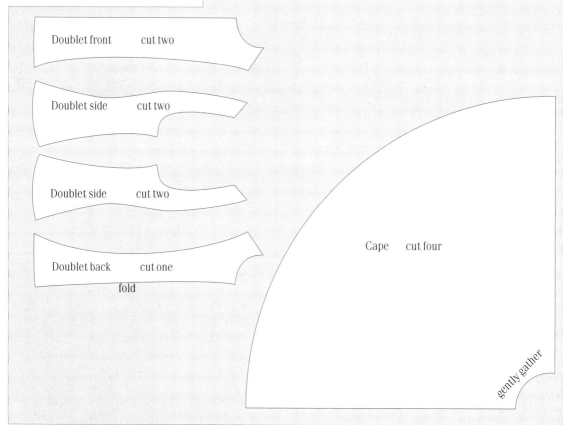

s with the man's shirt, generally
eeves were full and gathered and
llars were large. Skirts were wide
d gathered, worn over padding at
e waist but not severly hooped. This
sic shape applies to a Puritan ver-
on or dressier version. Courtly
esses were often off the shoulder
colleté whereas the Puritan ver-
ons were high and prim.

e choice of fabric is all impor-
nt–choose silks and satins for the
nate version or dark woollen
oth–perhaps an old blanket–for the
ritan version.

op

1 Cut out the bodice pieces as
shown on the right.

2 Join shoulder sections to front
and back bodice pieces.

3 Attach the front and back sections
of bodice to the side pieces.

4 Hem and finish all the edges and
add lots of ribbon trimmings and
ce on all the edges.

5 Then add a lace fichu or a soft
scarf of fabric and tie this in a bow
t the front or fix with an ornate
rooch or pin.

6 Sew sleeve side seams. Gather
the shoulder seam. Gather to
eate cuffs at the wrist.

7 Then attach sleeves in the usual
way to the bodice armhole.

8 You can cut slightly longer sleeves
and then gather above the elbow
r an extra flourish. Elastic or
ufflette tape might be used for this.

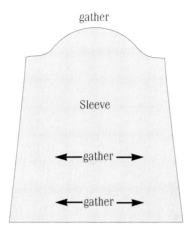

gather

Sleeve

←— gather —→

←— gather —→

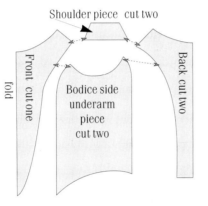

Shoulder piece cut two

Front cut one

fold

Back cut two

Bodice side
underarm
piece
cut two

Skirt

Make the skirt using a single length of
fabric gathered to fit the waist with either Rufflette curtain tape, elastic, or
a drawstring tied to fit.

Wear over hip pads or rolls.

Puritan version

For a Puritan style, the sleeves and
skirt can remain the same but do not
add any of the lavish trimmings or extra padding.

Either raise the neckline much higher
or make a simpler bodice and then
cover with a Puritan collar.

The Puritan effect will be completed
with the addition of a simple bonnet
and an apron.

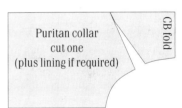

Puritan collar
cut one
(plus lining if required)

CB fold

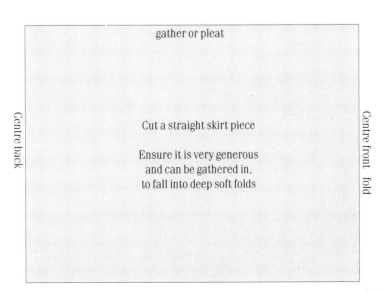

gather or pleat

Centre back

Centre front fold

Cut a straight skirt piece

Ensure it is very generous
and can be gathered in,
to fall into deep soft folds

A useful hint: using a chemise

Using the bodice pattern from the dress on page 111, make a simple chemise in plain fabric with long sleeves and a laced-up bodice. This can form the basis for many different costumes as a whole variety of skirts and bodices (with elbow-length sleeves, short sleeves, or no sleeves at all) can be placed over the top.

Accessories

Hats

A Puritan hat was severe and tall. This can be turned into a more exotic version for a cavalier with the addition of feathers and trimmings .

Caps and bonnets are generally worn by babies and children and by middle-aged and elderly women but are *de rigeur* for a Puritan lady, whatever her age. In time Quaker bonnets became quite extravagently detailed and already this is the one area in which a little femininity might occasionally be glimpsed.

See page 58 for instructions on how to make a bonnet and page 57 for instructions on how to make a tall Puritan hat.

A small lace or linen cap was often worn under another wider brimmed felt hat, the same as the men's in style.

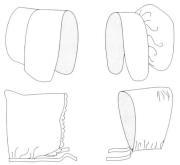

Shoes and gloves

Big buckles and bows or rosettes—on shoes with rounded or square toes and squat heels—the height of which increased as the century progressed. Often long front tongues sprouted behind the buckle.

Boots with lace cuffs: the lace can be real—or paper doilies—stuck onto canvas or Vilene with the scalloped edge overlapping so it can be seen.

Bedroom slippers or tap shoes can also be trimmed up.

Gloves became an important accessry, many becoming gauntlets wi flared lace extensions. See page 61.

Finishing touches

Lace, frills and feathers adorne clothing and hats alike.

Lace cravats and rippling frills ar flounces add flourish to a man's shi or lady's bodice.

Buckles, bows and rosettes decora waistlines, cleavages, necklines an hats as well as shoes.

Sashes and belts abound. Collars ar huge—lace ones for the fashion co scious; linen or cotton for Puritans.

Attach lace flounces to elastic to wea at the wrists—and knees for men.

Deep buttoned back cuffs on jacket Lots and lots of buttons appear c everything from jackets, cuffs, wais coats, sleeves and shoes, and ther are rows of large decorative buttor holes on men's clothes.

Frills, flounces and lace cravats add the right flourish.

This is the time of the French Revolution, of court fops and dandies, of powdered wigs and beauty spots, of highwaymen and tricorn hats and Gainsborough ladies. It is the setting for *A Tale of Two Cities* and *Cinderella*.

The poorer classes are dressed in ragged clothes and the working and servant classes in poorer versions of the rich styles, with aprons for both men and women.

Fabrics

Silk, satin and brocade, which have dominated the fashion scene, are still very popular but now are joined by the soft folds and flounces of muslin, lawn and organza. These are also used for many accessories–such as handkerchiefs and cravats–in the hair and as dainty decorative aprons.

Velvet is especially popular for men.

Men

Long curly wigs are replaced by white powdered ones, pulled back and tied with ribbons or encased in little silk bags drawn up with cords at the nape of the neck.

Jackets have lots of buttons and flare out from the waist.

Cravats and flounces can be sewn onto an old collarless shirt.

Lacy cuffs need to show at the wrist. Try spraying lace with gold or silver for a really exotic effect.

Waistcoats are in rich brocades and silks. The long styles gradually become shorter and the breeches more visible and therefore more ornate

Riding breeches, ski pants and jogging suits can be converted into leggings and breeches while old curtains and chintz can be turned into the more exotic versions.

Fine white tights or long white woollen socks should be worn under the breeches.

Huge buttons appear on the jackets.

Enormous decorated buckles on the shoes complete the effect.

Women

Dresses were now fitted to the waist and wide skirts often flare open at the front over a matching or a contrasting underskirt.

Sometimes a loose pleated central back section cascades from the neckline, as shown on the facing page.

Eventually these open skirts develop into the polonaise style with overskirts hooped up into swags to reveal decorative petticoats (See page 34 on how curtain tape can be used to achieve this effect.)

The look is the elegant beribboned shepherdess.

The dress should be worn over hoops or with paniers to suit this period, and with the skirt separated at centre front or pulled up into swags to reveal a tiered petticoat.

Accessories

Hats and hair

Tricorne hats are universal, whatever the class or sex, with mob caps for working women.

Ladies wear immense piles of hair.

Wigs are crowned with combs, little hats, lace and ribbon 'fontages' or huge organdie mob caps covered in decoration. (See also page 60.)

Feathers crown hair styles and hats.

Straw hats are popular, sometimes with a soft fichu of muslin or lawn, tied under the chin.

Shoe styles: heels are higher.

Fans are at their most elaborate and often encrusted with jewels.

Men's stockings: these are decorated and coloured at the beginning of the century but later become plain white silk and then wool.

Finishing touches

Intricate stitching and embroidery.

Big ornate buttons.

Extravagantly decorated and bejewelled buckles.

Pockets are not yet sewn into clothes. Insteads, hidden pairs of small pockets like drawstring purses are tied around the waist, and then reached through slits in the skirt.

False hips, hooped skirts and back-waist bustle padding create the domed shapes of the period.

Petticoats are often highly decorated and quilted–old satin bedspreads might be a useful source of fabric.

Lots of flounces cascade from elbow-length sleeves.

Miniatures are in vogue and tiny portraits adorn brooches and decorate little satin muffs.

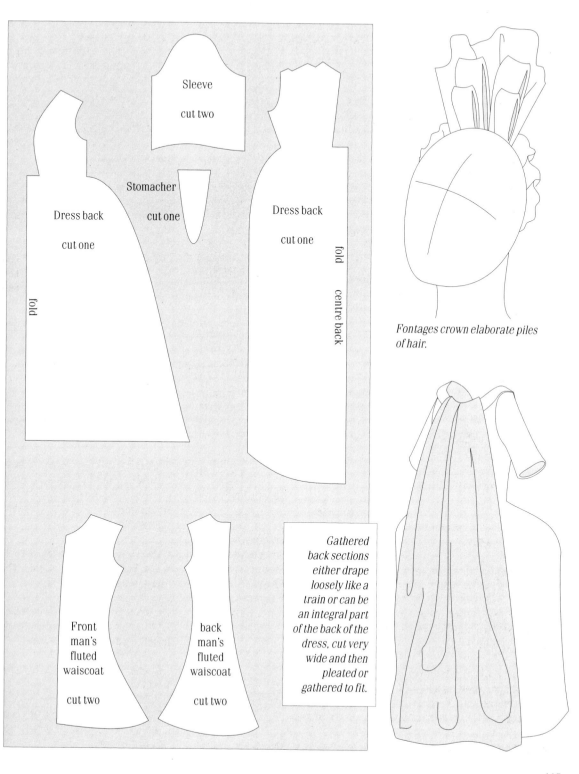

Sleeve

cut two

Stomacher

cut one

Dress back

cut one

fold

Dress back

cut one

fold   centre back

Fontages crown elaborate piles of hair.

Front man's fluted waiscoat

cut two

back man's fluted waiscoat

cut two

Gathered back sections either drape loosely like a train or can be an integral part of the back of the dress, cut very wide and then pleated or gathered to fit.

Early nineteenth century

Regency costumes

For a short relaxed interlude before the Victorian regime imposed its tight-laced corsets and wide skirts, there was a brief period when ladies escaped into flimsy high-waisted dresses worn with neither corset nor even petticoat underneath. For a while women wore loose flowing dresses in soft fabrics, which, free from any restricting undergarments, clung to their bodies.

This is the time of Napoleon, the Regency period, when Jane Austen's characters made visits to the spas to take the waters while the men's fashions were strongly influenced by the military activities taking place on the battlefields of Europe.

Double-breasted coats and rows of buttons or braiding reflect the influence of military uniforms.

Accessories

Big brimmed bonnets were popular.

Ladies carried parasols made of silk. and fur muffs to warm their hands

Use lots of ribbons, bows and sashes.

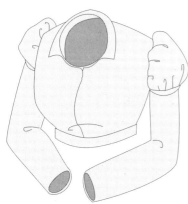

High waisted spensers were often worn over the dresses.

It is often also possible to convert soft flowing high-waisted nightdresses into dresses from this period.

Pattern pieces for the bodice of a simple high-waisted dress. Add a full-length skirt in soft fabric.

gather

Sleeve

gather

gather

CB

CF fold

gather

Bodice front

gather

Bodice front

gather

Victorian and Edwardian England

Early Victorian dress from the middle of the 19th century

Edwardian gentleman at the turn of the century.

The sewing machine arrived in the middle of the nineteenth century and introduced mass production—both of clothes and of materials like lace.

Dress from the late nineteenth century.

Many Victorian and Edwardian men's clothes were, however, cut to fairly severe lines and highly tailored–and therefore they are not the easiest in the world to make with limited resources.

Ladies' skirts grew gradually wider to become, eventually, crinolines–and then the bustle arrived which, in varying degrees of bulk and position, dominated the designs from the 1870 to the turn of the century. At last, the lines became more relaxed again. The hour-glass figure was still sought but tight lacing, pads and hoops had gone as skirts flowed out gently.

You may, of course, be lucky enough to be given an old morning or frock coat or a riding habit from someone's attic turn-out or to discover an evening jacket at a jumble sale that can be converted with the addition of braid and tails.

The easier garments to make at home are cloaks and capes, breeches and waistcoats which will all help towards the period feel.

Blazers, too, are relatively easy to make and can look good trimmed with braid or in tweeds for country wear.

Ladies dresses are full of tucks and pleats but are not quite so difficult to contrive, especially as the conversion of blouses with masses of tucks and lace, combined with full skirts worn over hoops can often form the backbone of the costume requirements.

Servant girls need plain black skirts and pinafores and, for the poorer classes, keep a store of old bonnets and lots of woollen shawls–old blankets will serve.

See also the child's Victorian smock on page 49.

Early twentieth century gown.

Young woman's coat dress
(circa 1880)

A new collar, some velvet ribbon and plenty of ingenuity will convert an old cast-off coat into a fashionable Victorian garment.

You will need

A coat (preferably a semi-fitted coat which is not too bulky). If possible, select a coat which has no apparent design in the fabric. A single strong colour will have more impact.

Narrow velvet ribbon or bias binding. Make sure there is enough to trim the coat as illustrated. Use some string to sort out the length (do not guess or estimate!) and purchase a little extra, just in case!

Thread: to match the coat and the velvet bias trim.

Zip. An 'invisible zip is best for this, to give the impression of a 'butted' seam. The length should be from the neck to the hip, or just above. Remember: zip-fasteners were not invented until 1892, so do not spoil a period costume by using an obvious modern zip.

Lace. Pre-gathered broderie anglaise on a bias strip (enough to go round the neck and two cuffs.)

1 Remove any buttons and decorative features from the coat, unpicking where necessary and trimming away surplus fabric. Sew together (as invisibly as possible) any slash pockets or buttonholes. Hopefully these can be camouflaged by the later addition of trimmings.

This point should be approximately 8 inches (20 cm) longer than the zip.

2 Turn the coat inside out and fit it on the actress. Stand the collar and lapels up and pin the front openings together. The fit should be reasonably snug, to give a close-fitting appearance, although it is essential to allow the actress plenty of shoulder room so as not to hamper any movements. Trim away the surplus fabric as indicated.

3 If the sleeves are too wide, take them in from the cuff end, gradually decreasing the width of seam until armhole is reached.

4 Fit and sew the zip to the front opening of the coat and join the surplus material with a seam at the base of the zip.

Note if the coat is still not sufficientl fitted, it may be necessary to sev darts into the front and/or the back, a shown, to give a better line to the coa Pin whilst coat is inside out.

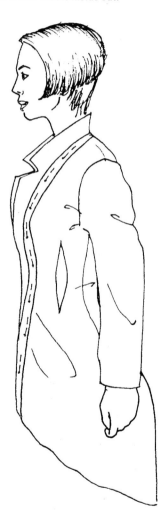

If you are lucky enough, there may be adequate material from the bottom o the coat to construct a collar; otherwise purchase some matching material or contrasting velvet.

5 Make a rough paper pattern of the collar to fit the actress. Trim this pattern whilst in position to obtain a correct fit. Fold the paper and trim off any unequal edges. This will make the collar balanced and symmetrical.

It is unlikely that you will have enough material to cut the collar in one piece. Instead, cut the paper pattern along the shoulder seam to divide it into three pieces, taking care to add extra for the seam allowance when actually cutting the fabric.

6 Encase outer edge with bias or, if using velvet ribbon, make a small single hem on the right side of the outer edge of collar. Top-stitch the velvet over this.

Note: Narrow velvet should be used, as wide ribbon would have to be darted or gathered to encompass the curves of the collar.

Mitre the trim at the corner.

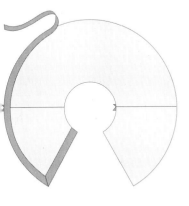

7 Place the right side of the collar and the wrong side of the coat's neck opening together. Stitch two rows here for reinforcement. Make sure the seam allowance is identical on each side so that the collar will sit evenly.

8 Pass running stitches through the centre front of the coat up to the zip base and then pull the thread to gather the fabric. Arrange the gathers with the coat lying on a flat surface, then back stitch on the inside of the coat to keep the drapery in position.

9 Sew hem on coat, incorporating lining (which should have been trimmed as necessary).

Trim away the shaded area.

10 Allow the drapes to drop gracefully towards the rear of the coat, using occasional bar tacks to keep folds in position.

11 The trim on the bodice and the sleeves can be placed as illustrated, although a certain flexibility of approach is perhaps needed here, as the trim may be required to cover up unwanted marks, pocket seams, or buttonholes.

12 To finish outfit, gathered broderie anglaise can be stitched just inside the neck and cuff edges giving the impression of a fashionable blouse underneath.

This type of coat can be teamed with a variety of full skirts in heavy fabrics such as velvet, corduroy and woollen weaves in a similar or contrasting fabric, perhaps relating to colours in the braid or trimming. The skirt can be cut in gores, pleated or gathered with greatest fullness at the back.

Edwardian lady's blouse

This blouse is made from a man's shirt, worn back to front. The detachable collar is sufficiently simple and versatile to be converted into a 'Puritan' collar, by turning it 45 degrees so it becomes square instead of triangular. (See next page.)

You will need

Man's shirt: Cotton or polyester and cotton, preferably white.

Lace: Use 0.75 metre (³/4 yard) of inexpensive cotton lace, or an old lace curtain.

Pre-gathered edging lace: Same length as collar measurement, plus 5-8 cm (2-3 in) extra.

Ribbon: Sufficient to encircle neck-edge and cuffs; can be a contrasting or co-ordinating colour, as suits the design.

Buttons: Three or four small ones

Fabric stiffener: Try the sort which is used to stiffen material for blinds.

1 Trim away the shaded area and cut off the sleeves at the elbows. Remove any pockets or epaulettes. Check the shirt's fit and overlap at the back if necessary. Resew the buttons to ensure a good fit, especially at the neck. Take in the sleeves if these are too baggy.

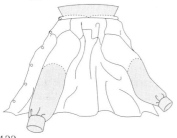

2 Slot in the pre-gathered lace between the two raw edges of the collar. Fold in the collar edges to neaten them and hem them to the lace, using small, stabbing stitches. Tuck the ends of the lace completely into the collar seam at the neck openings to hide raw edges.

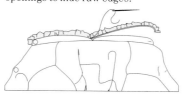

3 Measure the shoulder width of actress to determine size of lace square required. Allow about 8-10cms (3 or 4 in) extra so the collar will drape properly over the shoulders. Fold the square over twice. Then cut out neck hole and scallop the edges, as shown.

4 Open out the square and make a slash for the neck opening.

5 Cut out the cuffs, as shown. Spray collar and cuffs with fabric stiffener, paying particular attention to cut edges. This will help to prevent fraying and also gives the fabric more

body. Be sure to do this in a well ventilated room and then hang the lace out to dry.

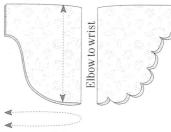

Diameter of sleeve
plus 2 inches

6 Sew cuff seams, joining the notches together. Tack cuffs into position on the shirt sleeves, and then sew ribbon over join to hide the seam, tucking in the raw edges. If these cuffs need to be detachable, finish off the shirt sleeve properly and attach cuffs with Velcro or snap fasteners.

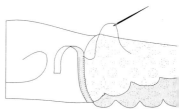

7 Bind neck-edge with remaining ribbon, extending this at one end to create a loop buttonhole. Sew on buttons and make cotton loop buttonholes, checking that the back edges of shirt stay exactly in line. Blanket stitch over the cotton loops to give them extra strength.

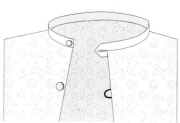

emember: the shirt must be worn ack to front!

he collar can be attached to the shirt ith loose bar tacks but then it will not e so readily detached or available to reate a different costume.

f the collar is worn in reverse, then ne shirt might also be converted into he top bodice section of a 1920s traight short dress

Accessories

Top hats are a vital ingredient.

The bowler arrived later, along with the **Sherlock Holmes style cap** which complements the breeches worn for casual or country wear. (See instructions on page 61.)

Straw boaters were very popular in the 1900s.

Women's demure **caps** and **bonnets** of early Victorian times give way to tiny lace veils; then feathers perched on top or cascading over hat brims. In Edwardian times, big **straw hats**, laden with fruit and flowers.

Parasols are very pretty–and often elaborately trimmed.

Dainty shoes–ballet shoes or little slipperettes will do.

Button boots–collect cast-off boots or buy them cheaply in sales–if all else fails, use dark socks over shoes, trimmed up with buttons.

Gaiters, for men and women, can be made of felt or suede-like fabrics or mock or chamois leather (see page 63). **Spats** are just a shorter version of these.

Gloves are always worn out of doors and lace or satin ones are essential for ladies' evening wear.

Finishing touches

Mourning in Victorian times, could dominate fashion decisions. Black or sombre colours were worn a great deal, as well as special black, gold and enamel jewellery and jet beads.

Cameo brooches and lockets abound, as do watches and chains for men and fob watches for ladies

Stiff upper necks! Rigid collars and cuffs–for men, women and servants; pearl chokers or velvet ribbons and hair piled up on top emphasised the Edwardian swan-like neck.

Feathers, lace and pearls were favourite decorative features in Edwardian times, as well as lots of pleats and pin tucks.

Leg of mutton sleeves abound.

Underwear

Lots of petticoats, then hooped crinolines and, finally, the S-shape corset and the bustle characterised the shapes of the Victorian and then Edwardian dresses. If some suitable petticoats and bustles can be contrived and made in good fabric they will last for years and be a very useful part of the wardrobe.

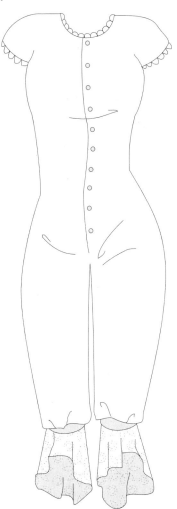

Pairs of combinations and bloomers are relatively easy to make and some styles can be useful as Edwardian bathing costumes too.

Changing decades 1920s

The First World War has a phenomenal effect on the role of women as their emancipation takes effect and they revoke both the political and the social shackles of previous centuries. Fashion reflects this revolution. In fact, the 'flapper' look is so totally different from 1910 that centuries seem to have passed rather than just one decade. Some of the older generation, however, still continue to wear longer skirts and corsets.

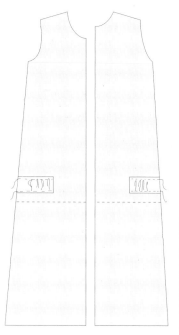

Simple pattern for a flapper dress. This basic style can be altered by cutting it short where indicated to make a straight top and then adding a short skirt—either bias cut, gathered or pleated.

Made in satin or crepe de chine - with perhaps fringes or beading—will turn this dress into Roaring Twenties evening wear.

Fabrics
Checks, spots and stripes are popular.
Silk
Crochet and knitted fabrics
Rayon

WOMAN

Mannish styles

Short skirts - which reach the knees by 1927

Hair cropped and shingled

Flat chests, and drop waists

Sleeveless blousettes, with a gathered waist

Ties and hip-length waistcoats

Wrap coats with a single low button

Waistcoats

V-neck sweaters

Skirts often have pleats and inserts

One-piece bathing costumes, usually in cotton

Flannel shorts

Accessories and underwear

Clasp and envelope shape handbags

Multiple rows of beads

Feather boas

Scarves and bandeaux

Ankle socks

Pale coloured stockings

Cigarette holders

Narrow ties

Jewellery

Pearls

Rows of beads

Tie pins

Costume jewellery - fake stones become fashionable

Hair and hats

Toques

Helmets and cloches, with or without brims

Cropped, bobbed and shingles

Shoes

Short 'lavatory' heels

Shoes in pale shades, often coloured to match outfits

Pointed toes

Straps, bows, buckles and buttons

Finishing touches

Deep collars, long and pointed

Fringes, beading and Egyptian-style embroidery

MEN

Striped sports jackets

Cream flannels

Oxford bags - at their widest by 1925

Double-breasted suits

Wide trousers with turn-ups

Plus fours

Dinner jackets

Stiff white shirts with stand-up collars for evening wear

Waistcoats

V-neck sweaters

One-piece bathing costumes

Flannel shorts

Early 'aviation' styles

Accessories

Cigarette holders

Monocles

Braces

Narrow ties

Diamond patterned socks

Silk cravats under open-necked shirts

Round spectacles with tortoiseshell frames

Breast pocket handkerchiefs

Hair and hats

Short 'oiled' hair

Cloth caps

Soft trilbys

Homburgs

Shoes

Country brogues

Flat-heeled lace-up 'Oxfords'

Evening - grey spats over patent leather shoes

Finishing touches

Deep collars, long and pointed

Changing decades 1930s

Femininity makes a comeback with curves reappearing. So does sophisticated, glamorous evening wear, perhaps inspired by the ever-increasing impact of Hollywood and the movies and the need for escapism–this is especially obvious in evening wear.

Despite the Depression, clothes are stylish and elegant. Casual holiday clothes arrive in force. The standards of mass-produced clothes is improving, especially in the USA, but many women still have to make their own and the clothes have to last a long time; home-knitted garments are extremely popular.

During the 1920s and 1930s sports and holidays became increasingly popular with strappy one piece bathing costumes worn by both

WOMEN

Breasts reappear and the waistline now returns to its normal position

Skirt lengths drop generally and are full length for evening wear: they are fluted or bias cut, often clinging to the hips before swirling out dramatically

Dipped and zig-zagged hems

Low-cut, backless evening dresses

Clothes inspired by hiking and sport activities - cricket sweaters and cardigans, Fair Isle V-necks

Knitted bathing costumes - sometimes with shoulder straps and holes under the armpits

Japanese-inspired styles such as kimono jackets, silk dressing-gowns, lounging suits and pyjamas

Fur trimmings

Built-up shoulders

Accessories

Big floppy bows at the neckline

Fox fur stoles with heads

Noel-Coward style silk dressing-gowns

Gloves to match outfits

Hand-knitted gloves

Jewellery

Rhinestone and diamanté ear-rings and matching clips

High pearl chokers

Finishing touches

Sweetheart necklines

Gathered and ruched sleeves

Ostrich feathers and sequins for evening wear

Lots of drapes, cowl necks and capes

Hats

Small jaunty hats perched at an angle or dipping over one eye

Berets

Tyrolean hats

Hats with tiny veils

Snoods and head scarves by the end of the decade

Shoes

Court shoes

Strappy open-toed sandals

High-heeled lace-up shoes

Ankle strap shoes

Platform soles

Fabrics

Generally quite subdued colours

Soft fabrics like wool and jersey

Evening - crepe de chine, soft shiny satin

MEN

Broad shoulders and wide revers

Long raincoats and overcoats (the 'gangster' look)

Finely striped double-breasted suits and waistcoats

Wide baggy trousers with turn-ups

Narrow striped shirts

High waists and corresponding high buttons and pockets

Striped blazers

First zip flies

Built-up shoulders

Accessories

Noel-Coward style silk dressing-gowns

Hand-knitted gloves

Braces hitching trousers quite high at the back

Striped cravats

Elastic suspenders

Baggy underpants and vests

Elastic arm bands holding up full sleeves

Finishing touches

Stud collars

Round spectacles

Hair and hats

Trilbys

Hair less oiled than the 1920s and although still short, slightly longer and wavy on top

Shoes

2-tone shoes–correspondents

Plain leather or canvas

Flat-heeled lace-ups

Toe and heel caps in black or brown leather

Top stitching

Loafers and mocassins in USA

Changing decades 1940s

Europe is at war. In some countries materials are scarce and clothes are rationed. People are either in the forces or coping as civilians–perhaps in civil defence, the land army, working in factories or at home looking after the children. The middle classes and rich can still afford fashionable hats (which are not rationed) and neat clean-cut tailored styles, especially in the USA where glamorous styles are also readily available. USA dominates the fashion scene. But many ordinary women's clothes are utilitarian and dowdy. Necessity is the mother of invention– clothes are often converted from men's suits when they are away fighting; dresses are updated by altering, and by dyeing or trimming.

After the war, in 1947, as a reaction to its restrictions, the Paris collections and Dior's New Look introduce generous flared skirts–up to twenty-five yards in one skirt–but in general, materials are still in short supply. Clothes are rationed in Britain until 1949. A more relaxed attitude to evening wear develops and gradually all clothes become less formal. South American styles and the popular tango dance inspire strong colours, bare midriffs and frills.

Fabrics

Cotton
Flannel
Gabardine
Lawn
Wool and knitting
Clear colours but with
black and navy
for smart
town clothes
Heavy duty materials
for uniforms

WOMEN

Wartime

At last trousers are acceptable

Boiler suits and overalls at work

Wrap-over pinafores

Square padded shoulders

Short fluted jackets

Waspee waists

Knitted cardigans and twin sets

Post-war

Suits with three-quarter length jackets and short box-pleated skirts

The New Look with long full skirts

Dirndl skirts

The Tube - with narrow shorter skirts

Elasticised swimwear - then the bikini arrives!

Ballet length dresses

Accessories

Large shoulder bags

Knitted gloves

Elbow length evening gloves

Wartime thick stockings

Jewellery

Often handmade during the war, using everyday items like corks, crochet and beads

Flower corsages or big brooches at waist or shoulder

Shoes

Wartime

Flat clumpy shoes

Post- war

Plain high-heeled court shoes in black leather or suede

Open-toed sling-backs with high heels Ankle straps. Elegant platform soles

Hats

Wartime

Snoods

Head scarves

Turbans

Balaclava helmets

Big berets

Black halo hats

After the war

Women wear neat head-fitting shapes trimmed with ribbons or feathers

Large straw summer hats

Pill boxes

Finishing touches

Seamed stockings - draw in lines on tights, if necessary

Ruching at the bust

Waists belted

MEN

Wartime

The young men are generally in the forces until 1945

Combat suits and uniforms

Uniforms at home - Civil Defence etc

Loose jackets and coats

Post war

Demob suits

Straight wide trousers

Padded shoulders

Sheepskin-lined flying jackets

Wide collars and revers

Accessories

Wartime

Knitted gloves

Wide ties

Post war

Shoes

Wartime and Post- war

Round toes

Hair and hats

Wartime

Balaclava helmets

After the war

Young men do not wear hats

Handlebar moustaches

Crew cuts

Changing decades 1950s

For the young–the 'call-up' to armed forces means that young men are often in uniform; the younger generation meet up in coffee bars, listening to juke boxes and sporting pony tails and jeans.

The older generation still dress very conservatively, and are often referred to as 'square'.

Women's hair is dressed in French pleats or in very short waved styles. Overall, the bust is big news and emphasised by pointed bras, falsies and sculptured raised cleavages. Waists are also in fashion, emphasized by wide belts nipping in full circular skirts made more pronounced by layers of net underskirts. The hemline is generally mid-calf. According to their taste, women might emulate Marilyn Monroe or Audrey Hepburn, Grace Kelly or Bridgitte Bardot. Rock and roll, skiffle and beatniks dominate the pop music scene.

Fabrics

Natural fabrics
Cotton
Wool
Tweeds
Mohair
Jersey
Gingham
Broderie anglaise
Gaberdine
Flannel
Synthetic fabrics (late fifties)
Terylene
Acrilan
Bri-Nylon
Orlon
Spots and lines and
informal patterns
Fairly conservative colours for
day wear, especially sombre
for winter clothes

WOMEN

Circular skirts worn over layers of net petticoats

Pencil tight skirts, with back slits or kick pleats

The sheaf dress

Wide swinging coats

Ball gowns for evening wear

Pedal pushers or tight trousers with ankle slits

The sack dress (1957)

Shirtwaister dresses

Jeans

Long sloppy jumpers

Pointed bras

Accessories and underwear

Wide belts

Evening stoles

Nylon stockings

Suspender belts, panty girdles and roll-ons

Highly decorative spectacle frames

Coloured umbrellas

Jewellery

Stud-shaped earrings

Brooches on lapels

Shoes

Flatties for 'rock and roll'

Stiletto heels and pointed toes

Usually black, brown or tan for winter (sometimes red), white or navy for summer

Sandals for summer

Hair and hats

Wide brims give way to tiny brimless hats

Pancakes and coolies

Small pill boxes with bows and nets

Bouffant back-combed hair by end of fifties

Finishing touches

Big pockets

Lots of darts

Half-belts on suits, coats and dresses

Pale face make-up ; heavy eye make-up by late 50s

MEN

Check shirts

Tailored waisted suits with high fastening revers and side or centre back vents

Tapered trousers

Camel coats

Duffel coats

Black leather jackets

Coloured and dark shirts were worn as well as white ones

Jeans

Long sloppy jumpers

Teddy boys

Drainpipe trousers

Velvet collar jackets

Velvet cuffs and trims on pockets

Winkle-picker shoes

Fluorescent socks

Sideburns

Hair and hats

Hair waves

Brylcreamed hair

Shoes

Crepe-soled shoes

Winkle-pickers

Pointed toes

Chunky blade shoes

Navy lace-ups with crepe soles

Accessories

Fluorescent socks

Narrow square-ended ties

Changing decades 1960s

The Swinging Sixties sees an explosion of clothes designed specifically for the young–both for the fashion-conscious males and the dusty-eyed false-eyelashed 'dolly birds'. The Beatles (and Beatle haircuts) rage as does Carnaby Street, with London the swingiest city of all. Colour returns with a vengeance–bright and courageous. Beehive hairstyles reach extreme heights, sometimes with heavily lacquered 'flick-ups', but then disappear as long straight hair or hair piled on top in curls takes over. There are mods and leather-clad rockers: Jean Shrimpton and Twiggy. Surfing becomes a cult sport. By 1967 hippies and flower power arrive with a strong Indian influence in styles and fabric.

WOMEN

Mini skirts - the 'pelmet'

Very short mini dresses

Fitted bodices and bell skirts for evening wear or the little black dress

The Chanel suit with open front and braided edges

Stretched stirrup trousers

Smocks - the 'little girl' look

Trouser suits

Caftans from 1967

The maxi coat arrives in 1969

Unisex fashions

Hipster jeans and cowboy boots

Skin-tight jeans, shrunk to fit

Bright coloured shirts

Mix and match separates

Skinny rib sweaters

MEN

Collarless Beatles jackets

Jeans and leather jackets

Single-breasted short jackets

Duffel coats

Slim shirts with small collars

Pointed white collars on check, striped or plain coloured shirts

Short 'motoring' coats

Narrow trousers without turn-ups

Hipster trousers

Frilled evening shirts

Unisex fashions

Skin-tight jeans, shrunk to fit

Bright coloured shirts

Mix and match separates

Skinny rib sweaters

Polo necks

T-shirts

Anoraks

Loose Indian-style cotton shirts

Hats

Not generally worn except floppy caps for teenagers

Shoes

Slip-ons

Hippy sandles

1930s look and platforms

Thick soles

Finishing touches

Large fancy buttons

Turtle necks

Big floppy or pointed collars

Trousers all have zip flies not buttons

Indian-style beads

Polo necks

T-shirts

Anoraks

Loose Indian-style cotton shirts

Shoes

High boots - up to the knee or the thighs - stretchy with zips, or suede

Coloured shoes with chunky heels and square chisel toes

Patent leather with buckles

'Scholls'

Hats

Helmets

Dolly bonnets

Dr Zhivago fur hats and fur bonnets

Plastic rain hoods

Big brimmed floppy hats

Jewellery

Dangling plastic ear-rings - usually clip-ons

Pendants

Lots of Eastern style beads

Bracelets

Plastic popper beads

Indian-style beads

Accessories and underwear

Baby doll pyjamas

Tights arrive - plain, white, lacy, patterned, lurex - and seamless

Patent leather handbags with chain handles

Indian-style beads

Chiffon scarves

Chain belts

Fabrics

Corduroy

Silky evening fabrics

Small-flowered prints

Strong plain colours

Knitted stripes

Crochet

Cheesecloth

Finishing touches

Large fancy buttons

Smocking

Halter-neck, stand-up collars and turtle necks

Big floppy or pointed collars

Wigs are popular

Indian-style embroidery

Colourful psychedelic swirls and patterns

Special projects Nativity

Nativity plays are generally performed by young children so the clothes must be uncluttered and comfortable. There is nothing more distracting than a child who is fidgeting because the elastic around the waistline is too tight or a crown is in imminent danger of tumbling to the ground.

Choosing a style

Is is not always essential to stick to the predictable costumes and it can be interesting to try another slant.

The style of a nativity play might be based on any of the following:

Classic Biblical robes, with loose flowing head-dresses
Medieval styles as worn in miracle plays
The angular images and strong colours suggested by stained-glass windows
Renaissance or Victorian romantic paintings of the Nativity

Virgin Mary

Mary must look demure and gentle. Her head must be covered. She will need to wear a nun-style wimple or a veil or a robe draped over her head. She might have a halo–or, especially for a medieval or for a stained-glass window style, a crown.

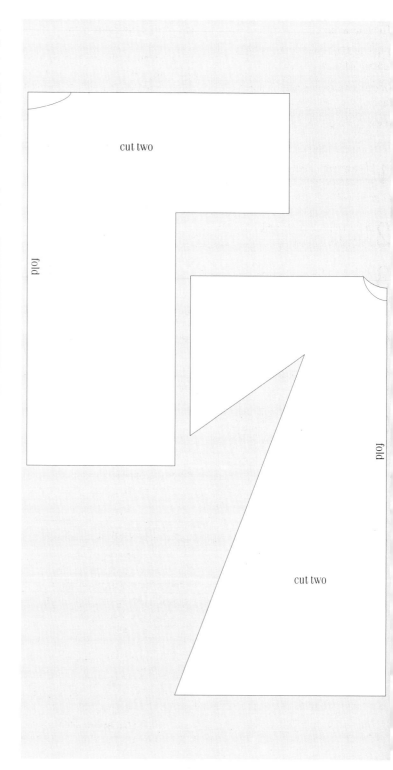

Simple patterns for biblical costumes. The one with wide sleeves is suitable for Mary, a king or an angel. The one with straight sleeves would suit Joseph and the shepherds– make it longer for Joseph.

To make a halo.

This can be piece of card, covered in foil or gold spray

Or card or foam covered in gold fabric.

It will need elastic to hold it in place.

1 Measure the child's head at the eyebrows and add 2.5 cms (1 inch) to this dimension.

2 Draw a circle the size of the final dimension on to paper.

3 Draw a second concentric circle which is 7.5cms (3 inches) bigger than the first.

4 Narrow the shape of second circle at base as shown.

5 Use this pattern to make halo in required materials.

6 Add elastic so that halo fits snugly on child's head, with the elastic worn under the chin or a the back of the head. Do make sure the elastic is comfortable—secure but without biting into the skin.

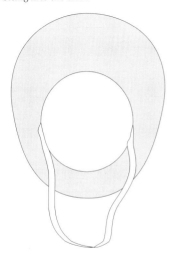

Joseph and the shepherds

Although these will be dressed in similar Biblical tunics and robes, it will be more interesting to make them—and for the audience to watch—if there are a few variations. A young shepherd boy might be in a simple rustic tunic, without a head-dress, carrying a lamb and a crook, while older shepherds and Joseph can wear longer robes, swathed over the head or with an Arab-style head-dress and an elasticised band or tied bandeau. One might simply wear a cloak over a tunic.

The Greek and Roman sections in this book show different ways of making and draping tunics and robes to form some basic Biblical costumes. Try to make them in different colours, in plain and in striped fabrics.

Variations

Fabric could be draped as shown on pages 86 and 89.
Use long or short tunics.
A dalmatic shape has
conical sleeves
Try a cloak, with or without a hood.
A wrap-around bath robe might also
serve, worn over a tunic.

Possible sources of material

Cotton or linen
Household linen: sheets,
tablecloths, tea towels, curtains
Bathrobes, towels or towelling
Blankets
Hessian

You will also need:

Elastic
Cord or braid for head-bands and
waist ties
Rope soles or sandals
(see page 62)

Kings

Try to dress the kings in different ways and colours, perhaps to reflect the three gifts they carry. They can either be regal kings, complete with cloaks and crowns, or wise men in Arabic or Eastern dress, wearing turbans or other Middle East or Oriental head-dresses. Rich colours and fabrics will help to suggest finery and form a sharp contrast to the rustic shepherds' clothing.

Crown suggestions

Try to make three distinctly different crowns so that each of the kings has an individual character.

For example, a crown might be a simple cardboard ring covered in gold paper or a turban can be built up with swathes of papier maché over a balloon (see page 45).

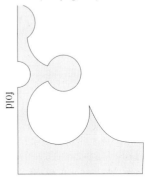

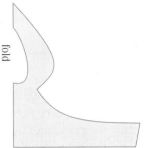

See page 59 for further information on how to make crowns.

Angel

The angel can be simply dressed in a long tunic with flowing or fluted sleeves, using the type of shape suggested on page 134.

Alternatively, a Christmas-tree doll effect can be achieved by using layers of net or chiffon and adding gold or silver tinsel trimming, stars of various sizes, glitter, ric-rac or braid.

Wings

Wings can be suggested most simply by wide tunic sleeves. Alternatively, a wide tunic or cape can be cut into a scalloped wing pattern .

Most commonly, they are made of wire with fabric or net stretched over.

They can have a softer feathery outline. This might be made of card–or

with a shiny fabric like satin–which is then stuffed with soft fibrefill batting (or kapok) and held in place with an elastic figure of eight.

Wings can be made of fabric suspended from the sleeves or from elastic around the wrists .

Angel wings, however, can be stylised, made of card, and worn with arm straps like a rucksack.

Wing pattern: Draw in lines on card wings as shown. Or overstitch fabric wings to achieve a quilted effect.

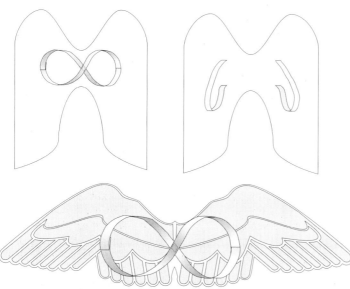

Both stylistic medieval wings and conventional angel wings can be kept in place with arm straps or figure of eight loops.

Stars can be represented by a head-dress cut to the shape shown or the entire body might be dressed as a star.

The Star

It is fun to include the star as a char-acter. The star costume might cover the entire body. Alternatively, a star can be suggested very effectively by using an open-faced mask (see page 80). Make a full-size star costume by using a card sprayed gold or silver or foam rubber that is covered in silver or gold fabric. Glitter might be added to give a truly sparkling effect.

Making the star (or a halo) glitter

1 First dilute half a cup of white glue into one or two tablespoons of water.

2 Apply the diluted glue to the wings with a brush.

3 Sprinkle glitter over the sticky surface before the glue dries.

4 Allow to dry and then shake off excess glitter.

5 Optional: Apply sequins, either gluing individually, using a hot glue gun, or sewing onto fabric.

Animals

The animals in the stable can be de-picted by children dressed up but any pantomime hilarity would, of course,

be inappropriate so it can be good to use masks of some kind, to suggest an ox or a mule, a camel or a horse. See pages 72-77 for more animal ideas.

Visitors to the stable

Some productions adhere strictly to the story according to the Gospels but the Christmas message can be con-veyed in further ways in order to involve lots more children in the per-formance. For example, there can be any number of visitors to the stable, bearing gifts, including children from all the nations of the world, or through history up to today, or Roman sol-diers, various animals and saints.

Fairy tale and pantomime

Fairy tale and fantasy, magic and pantomime: these can provide the most exciting opportunities for an enthusiastic wardrobe department, a time for escapism and extravagance. A wedding dress for a finale or a ball dress for Cinderella need to look simply wonderful but there are ways to achieve this without breaking the budget–and even if you are tempted to 'splash out' a little, usually this kind of production can bring in good income and merit a little extra expenditure.

Analyse the costume requirements carefully, discuss the budget and then decide which elements require most work and/or most money. Generally there is a balancing act between the two–cash versus energy and time–but it is important, whatever way the costs and work load are eventually distributed, that the audience are not let down in such a production, that the exotic can dazzle them occasionally and the magic be reinforced by inventive use of costumes and colour.

Convertible costumes

With a view to future use, and economy, many costumes can be made to fill a variety of roles–for example:

A body suit in fur fabric can be turned into all sorts of different animals if it has separate heads.

Short green medieval tunics can be suitable for Robin Hood and his Merry Men, Peter Pan, Dick Whittington and other medieval characters.

Circular cloaks can be 'zipped' together with Velcro to form a skirt.

A sweeping robe

Made in a suitable choice of fabric, with the edges cut out differently and with a variety of possible trimmings,

this shape robe will suit all kinds o fairy-tale and fantasy characters, including wicked queens, witches, a Princess, a medieval maiden, a wizard or an old hag .

Dame

A dame is the classic comic female character played by a man. The clothes will need to be as 'over the top' as the character, reflecting the comic burlesque role. Often there is a striptease scene when layers of silly clothes and undergarments add to the humour–everything from strings of sausages, long striped socks, hats piled up with paraphernalia to wild bloomers and huge corsets.

Typical dames include

Dame Twankey in
Aladdin,
Mother Goose,
the Cook in
Dick Whittington,
The Ugly Sisters in
Cinderella,
Mrs Crusoe in
Robinson Crusoe,
Dame Trot in
Jack and the Beanstalk
and The Queen of
Hearts in *Puss in Boots*
and *Alice in
Wonderland.*

She may require a pair of falsies. This is usually achieved by giving a large-sized bra false backs and then 'stuffing' the cups with foam or kapok. Meanwhile, up above, a dame's hat can be a wild extravagance, with all sorts of objects piled on top. Below, a crinoline skirt can hide all manner of funny objects like hot water bottles and a rolling pin. Long colourful knickers add to the humour.

Animal characters

Animal characters add a lot of fun to a pantomime and can be appealing or comic or both. Children in the audience love them and it can be a challenge for both actors and wardrobe to create. If your society or school presents lots of pantomimes, whenever the opportunity arises, try to build up stocks of costumes.

Animals in pantomime

Jack's cow in *Jack and the Beanstalk*

Pets including various dogs and cats–such as Puss in Boots or Dick Whittington's cat.

Exotic animals like lions in *The Wizard of Oz* or *The Lion, the Witch and the Wardrobe,* lots of beasts in *Jungle Book* or the camel in *Aladdin.*

Farm creatures like cows, horses, hens, pigs, or the goose in *Mother Goose.*

Woodland and water creatures like foxes, squirrels, frogs, toads–and all the animals that might appear in Beatrix Potter tales or *Toad of Toad Hall.*

Hints on making animals

Pick out and exaggerate the most striking features of any animal.

Puss in Boots or Dick Whittington's cat is an upright character and can be dressed in a suitable coloured all-in-one body which might be loose-fitting or a leotard. The boots and head are the main features but if the actor is to talk, or sing, an open-faced head will be essential.

You can make an elephant's trunk by covering plastic vent hose with fabric. See page 77.

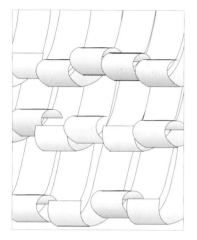

Goose feathers can be made from curled paper. Pull the paper tightly over the back of a ruler. When it is released it will spring into a curl.

For details on making lots of animal costumes see pages 72-77.

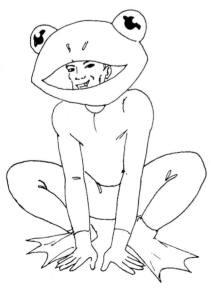

The important elements of a frog or toad are his wide mouth, huge eyes and splayed feet.

Principal boys

Generally these are played by an actress with good figure so the costume should reveal her legs. This hero may begin the play as a poor long-suffering young man with many trials ahead of him but will usually end up rich and successful and marrying the Princess. This will mean swopping a simple tunic or rustic outfit for satin and lace in the finale. Make the contrast extreme, with as much glamour as possible for the final flourish. Well known principal boys include Dick Whittington, Robin Hood, Aladdin, Jack (the giant-killer) and Prince Charming.

The heroine (principal girl)

Ideally, she should be dressed pretti-ly—as the sweet young innocent char-cter. Like Cinderella, she may be poor at the beginning or she might be a princess like Sleeping Beauty. No matter what her status, she should al-ways appear charming and appealing. Typical heroines include Little Red Riding Hood, Princess Badroubaldour in *Aladdin*, Cinderella, Beauty in *Beauty and the Beast*, Maid Marion in *The Babes in the Wood*, Alice Fitzwarren in *Dick Whittington* and the Sleeping Beauty.

From rags to riches

The classic Cinderella-style gown and Principal Boy wedding regalia can be based on the Restoration-style cos-tumes shown on pages 113-15.

Whatever the characters of principal boy and girl, the costumes in the finale

should be glamorous and create a dra-matic contrast to any poor or rustic costumes worn earlier. The audience need to go away remembering a final colourful or exotic 'splash'!

This effect can be helped by using some of the following

Shiny fabrics like silk and satin, or lining material

Glittery fabrics like lurex or lamé

Rich fabrics like velvet or brocade—old curtains, perhaps?

Lots of lace and flounces

Ribbons and bows

Sequins

Gold and/or silver—this can be sprayed on—spray lace with metallic paint; it looks very rich and effective.

Final finery—Cinderella (right) and Dick Whittington (left) before and happily ever after.

The Fairy

The goodies can include the traditional pantomime Good Fairy, obviously recognisable in glittering costume, wearing wings and coronet and waving a magic wand.

Alternatively, the fairy can be less obvious and without the sparkle when she appears as a fairy godmother or an old lady gathering wood in the forest. (Adapt the Sweeping Robe costume on page 138.)

She might also be disguised as a gypsy who turns the tide of fortune for the hero and heroine–bright colours, a bolero or a laced bodice, lots of ric-rac braid, a head scarf, shawl and big gold ear-rings will create a gypsy image.

The classic fairy wears a tutu of net or a long ballerina dress. Using layers of different coloured net can be very ef-

fective. For the longer version, a frill can be added at the bottom of the skirt–this can be made of more net, gathered at the top or the centre. A satin bodice with wings attached will complete the fairy costume and can be attached to the tutu. However, making the bodice independently will allow the longer style skirt to be used for other roles later–perhaps a princess or a cabaret singer.

Various different ways to make wings are explained on pages 74 and 136. Alternatively, simply gathering a stiff square of net in the centre like a big bow and attaching to a bodice can be a quick and easy method.

Both a fairy and a princess might wear a coronet. These can be made from wire threaded through tubular braid or from a wire foundation bound with tape. Either structure can then be decorated with sequins, stars, flowers, beads, pearls or whatever is appropriate. Old jewellery can be a useful source of adornment. Single earrings that have lost their partner can at last be put to good use!

The classic fairy wears a ballerina style costume but a skirt can be cut out in petal shapes for a flower fairy!

Baddies

The embodiment of evil, baddies may be dressed in strong colours, often reds, greens, black or purple. Glowing sequins or florescent paint that catch the light can help the magical effect. The general impression of evil is aided and abetted by a swirling cloak and an evil mask or grotesque make-up.

Typical baddies include the Demon King in *Mother Goose*, King Rat in *Dick Whittington*, the Wolf in *Little Red Riding Hood*, the Queen in *Snow White*, Uncle Abanazar in *Aladdin*, the Witch in *Hansel and Gretel*, the Sorcerer in *Sinbad the Sailor* and the Sheriff of Nottingham in *Robin Hood*.

Two archetypal pantomime baddies. See also page 150 for a demon

Demons will probably be in tights. A head-dress–hairy, horned or with exaggerated or contorted features- can have a strong visual impact and will help to create some of the more fantastic roles.

A pattern for a cloak or cape–useful for many pantomime characters–can be found on page 110.

Chorus and crowds

Both in pantomimes and musicals, it is important that any chorus, crowds or dancers are dressed well, in co-ordinated styles and colours when appropriate. Their impact is especially important when en masse, as the shapes and colours can fill the stage. This is not to say that they need always be identical: that can be boring, but an overall theme can add an extra element to any crowd scene.

Consider using the following

A range of related shades
or colours
perhaps many different greens

or all the colours in a bunch
of anemones

or rainbow shades, gradually
fading into each other from one
costume to the next.

You could try a variation of checks

or spots

or stripes

All these elements could be in
different sizes and/or colours.

Bright primary colours
for example, shiny shirts for the
men and vivid skirts for the girls

or sweet pastel colours

or everybody in black and white

Frills and flounces

Straight narrow lines

or full rounded skirts and sleeves

Wavy lines and scallops

or sharp edges and zig-zags.

There might be a stylistic option,–for example, costumes made of 'leaves' for a forest scene or shell shapes for an underwater sequence.

Some stories, like *Robinson Crusoe* or *Treasure Island*, might require a chorus of girls in flower garlands and grass skirts. These can be made from string, raffia, strips of tinsel or braid looped over a waist band of elastic or tape. They are not entirely concealing and should be worn with matching coloured briefs or leotards or bathing costumes underneath. Alternatively, a wrap-around sarong can be worn.

To make paper flowers

You will need

Green crepe paper for the leaves
and stamens

Different coloured crepe paper
for the flowers

Adhesive

Sewing thread

Scissors

1 To make the flowers, cut 3.5cm (1³/₈ inches) sections of the folded coloured crepe paper, as shown below. Unfold the sections and divide these into 40cm (16 inch) lengths. Gently stretch one long edge of each crepe paper section so that it begins to curve.

2 To make the stamens, cut 3.5 cm (1³/₈ inches) sections of folded green crepe paper, as shown above. This time keep the sections folded and snip one edge into points as shown below.

3 Then unfold and cut up into small lengths (about four points for each piece).

4 To make the leaves, cut 5cm (2 inch) sections of the folded green crepe paper. Keep the sections folded and snip one edge into curved arch points as shown. Then unfold and cut up into small lengths (about four points for each piece).

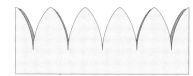

5 Glue the straight unsnipped edge of the stamen pieces to the unstretched edges of flower sections.

6 Roll up the flower and stamen sections, pleating and gathering the unstretched edges to form flower heads with the stamens in the centre.

7 Now wrap the uncut edge of the leaf strips around the base of the flower heads.

8 Bind the base of each complete leaf and flower head with thread.

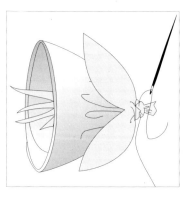

These flowers can be threaded together to make a garland or they can be used for head-dresses or bouquets or as buttonholes. Obviously the colours of the flowers and stamens should be chosen to suit the costumes and scenic effect.

Paper flowers look very effective and will last well if looked after properly by the actors and then packed away carefully and protected from crushing, strong sunlight or damp.

Instructions for making fabric flowers can be found on pages 67-9.

Grass skirts and sarongs

String or raffia can be looped or tied and then stitched together to create a grass skirt.

Sarongs can be long or short. Simply drape a long piece of fabric and knot at the hip, or gather and attach to an elastic waistband or a pair of briefs.

The thought of Oriental and Eastern dress summons up images of silks and brocades, Aladdin and *The Mikado*, willow-pattern plate designs, dragons, rickshaws and *The King and I*.

Fabrics have wonderful colours and patterns–often based on natural wildlife patterns and shapes–exotic flowers, butterfly wings, peacock feathers, herons, grasses, blossom.

Of course, these are all stereotyped images but even if your play is set in the back streets of Vietnam or war-torn Singapore, some shapes remain the same– baggy wide trousers and knee-length jackets with mandarin collars, for example.

Trousers for male or female are the same shape; a simple design, cut loose and gathered at the waist with elastic. The waistband will be covered by either the tunic or robe so it is not generally necessary to make them any more elaborate.

The robe or jacket are basically the same, with the robe cut longer. The distinctive features are the curved overlap front, fastened with toggles, and the neat mandarin collar. Made in pale blue or navy cotton or denim, these will serve as everyday 'street' costumes. Made in brocade, silk or out of a quilted satin bedspread, they will become rich costumes. Add braid and embroidery for an even more decorative finish.

Kimono

A kimono can be made from two oblongs of fabric, with wide sleeves. These sleeves can be cut very long to hang well below the wrists. The shawl 'collar' and edges of the kimono (or at least the visible parts on the side that wraps across) should be faced with a folded strip of fabric, often a contrasting colour or in a plain fabric to match one of the colours in a patterned kimono. Pattern shapes for a simple kimono are shown on page 146. For a more elaborate costume, the edges could also be finished with braid, ribbon or embroidery.

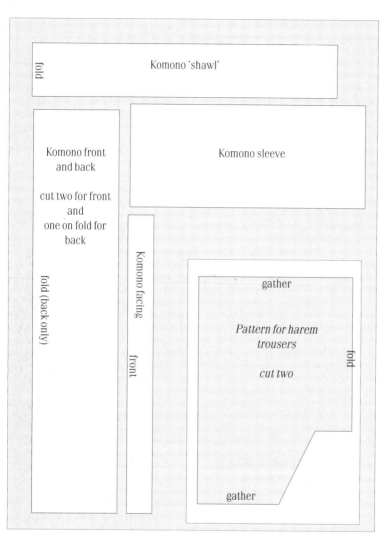

Komono 'shawl'

fold

Komono front
and back

cut two for front
and
one on fold for
back

fold (back only)

Komono sleeve

Komono facing

front

gather

*Pattern for harem
trousers*

cut two

fold

gather

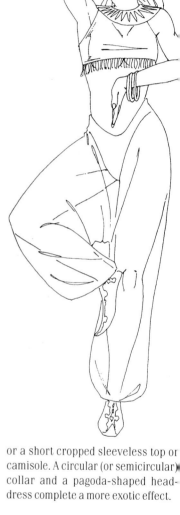

A wide sash, well stiffened to hold its shape, can be worn around the waist.

An extra wide sash should be worn higher and folded over at the back for a geisha style. Paper flowers in the hair look very effective. See page 144.

For any Chinese lady it is important to keep the feet looking as tiny as possible in small neat footwear. Although feet are no longer bound it is still considered important that feet look dainty. And a married lady would wear her hair in a plait coiled on top and kept in place with two ivory needles.

Harem outfit

Eastern dancers and harem wives wear simple low-crotch trousers, wide over the hips and narrow at the shins or ankles. These can be made up in silky or satin fabrics or semi-transparent net, net curtaining, muslin or gauze, with bikini briefs underneath. These trousers can be teamed up with a co-ordinating bikini top or a bolero or a short cropped sleeveless top or camisole. A circular (or semicircular) collar and a pagoda-shaped headdress complete a more exotic effect.

Alternatively, a veil and yashmak suggest an Arabian or Turkish lady. See also page 61 for how to make an oriental turban head-dress.

The feet are generally bare but medieval shoes, as described on page 62, with turned up toes might suit a Siamese or Balinese dancer.

Wild West

Lots of musical shows have a Wild West setting, for example, *Calamity Jane, Oklahoma,* or *Annie Get Your Gun.* Sketches, revues and plays are often given a Wild West flavour too. So it is useful to collect 'suitable' ingredients whenever these appear in jumble sales or charity shops or to make a note of them for future reference if, as often happens, these articles are already lurking in the wardrobe under some other guise:

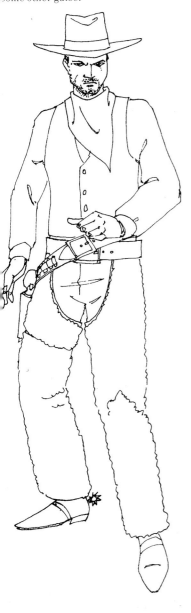

Wild West costume ingredients

Old jeans or dungarees

Plaid and check shirts

Waistcoats

Cowboy hats

Cowboy-style boots, or any that are suitable for conversion

Children's toy guns and ammunition belts, spurs and sheriff's star badges

Scarves, cravats and neckerchiefs

Braces

Leather belts

Any leather or suede fabric or old clothes that can be cut up

Fur fabric

Sheepskin

Old blankets and rugs car rugs and the hairy sort (they are all good for making shawls or capes and Indian costumes)

Feathers

Beads and silver buttons

Any source of fringing

Ric-rac braid

Cotton checks and gingham fabric for girls' frocks

Straw bonnets

Ribbons

Shawls (triangular ones or squares that can be folded into a triangle)

White sunbonnets

Cowboy

Most people can provide a pair of jeans for themselves as a starting point but they are not always an appropriate style. The secret then is to make chaps to wear over these– in fur, leather, suede, sheepskin–or any imitation of these. Pockets can be added, if required.

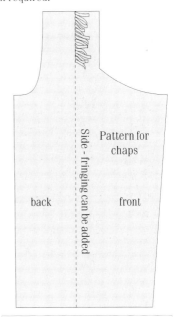

Side - fringing can be added

Pattern for chaps

back   front

Useful tips

Sheriffs always seem to wear a waistcoat or bolero.

A smart dark waistcoat combined with a fob watch and chain is ideal for the Western gent.

Braces or dungarees, combined with check shirts and straw hats, look good for country folk and old timers.

Most wide brimmed hats in felt or straw can be converted into a cowboy hat. They need a dent in the crown and then the brims can easily be steamed into the right shape.

Native American Indian

An Indian can be dressed in simple loin cloth aprons or a well-fringed tunic and leggings. Any animal skin fabrics like fur and leather are good but expensive; old rugs and blankets or felt may provide a good substitute. Felt is especially good because it does not fray when fringed but if the blanket material is sized or stiffened, it can then be cut up in the same way.

These plain fabrics can be painted in Indian designs–diamonds, ethnic patterns, buffalo or eagle designs. Many braids have the right colours and designs and a wide strip of suitable braid can transform an old blanket into something suitably tribal.

Large swathes of fabric, big shawls or an old blanket can be draped over the shoulder rather like a Roman or Greek toga. Beads, teeth and bone substitutes (card, papier maché, polystyrene) can be used for trimming and for rows of necklaces.

Feathers can be collected or bought or made.

Sources of feathers include

Bird's feathers in the countryside, park, garden or the zoo

Gull feathers at the seaside

Poultry suppliers

Old pillows– too small and light for a head-dress but sometimes useful for decoration

Craft shops

Florists

Generally it may be easier to make imitation ones out of buckram or several layers of strong paper or crepe paper.

Making feathers

1 If necessary, paint fabric or paper the required colour: allow to dry.

2 Make a pattern of the basic feather profile and pin this to fabric. The ragged edges will give a good guideline for regular slashing.

3 Mark centre vein and slash down to within 1/4 inch (7mms) of this.

4 Attach millinery wire to make a flexible centre spine, sandwiched between the layers of paper, or catch with herringbone stitches if fabric.

5 Paper feathers can be curled by holding paper very firmly so it is under tension and then drawing it over a sharp blade.

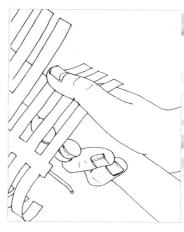

Mexicans

The Mexican style is heavily influenced by the Spanish invaders as shown in the strong colours, short 'matador' jackets and mantilla head-dresses. Shirts for men and women can be of silk or some slick shiny fabric. A long cape or pocho–perhaps with stripes–and a big sombrero are prerequisites to create a convincing Mexican atmosphere.

Women

Cowgirls can be dressed in similar materials to their male counterparts but might opt for a fringed skirt instead of jeans, and a bolero rather than a waistcoat.

With the Puritan influence dominating the early settlers, ladies' clothes were simple versions of the seventeenth and eighteenth-century styles,

with full hooped skirts and bonnets and aprons. Gingham frocks with white collars and straw bonnets will suit a group of young girls.

Saloon girl

This a chance for extravagance–bold colour, feathered head-dresses, a can-can skirt, lots of frilled petticoats, suspenders and a feather boa. The bodice will need to be low-cut and

Gossards Wonderbra will come into its own! The costume should be a complete contrast to the Puritain styles.

Squaws

Squaws need a simple long tunic over trousers or a fairly straight or wrap-around skirt. Hair can be plaited and strings of necklaces and bracelets of beads or shells add detail and interest to the final impression.

Two contrasting wild west women: A saloon girl and a squaw.

Monsters, myths and science fiction

Creating a monster is quite a challenge and may need the combined forces of the wardrobe, properties, special effects and the make-up teams. Much depends on whether the head–assuming the creature has a head–is to be the actor's own or a mask. Earlier sections in the book have described the practicalities of making masks and using papier maché (see pages 45, 78-83 and 85) so the intention here is to explore all the possibilities, to 'brainstorm', to unlock the inventiveness that such an open-ended subject can promote. These roles are all figments of the imagination, the stuff of fantasy, dreams and nightmare, so it is a wonderful opportunity to escape the normal bounds and to experiment.

Having said that, there are always stereotyped images, of course, even for the unreal–sheet-like ghosts and long-fanged vampires, to name but two–and there are occasions when, for reasons of clarity and instant recognition–these familiar forms are, in fact, the best options.

Anyway, here are a few how to's and ideas. The ways in which the various elements are brought together is entirely up to your imagination!

Nightmare material

A portrait gallery of well-known ghouls, monsters and mythical creatures in any book on the horror film genre or a children's book on monsters will provide vivid inspiration.

Meanwhile, on the right and on page 151 are a few suggestions for interesting monsters, their particular features and, in some cases, how these effects might be achieved.

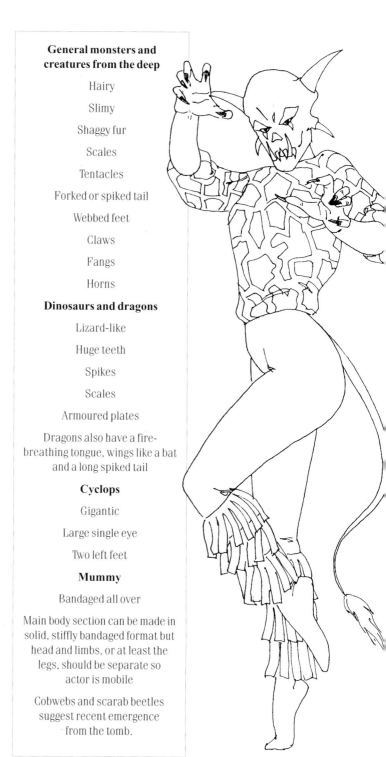

General monsters and creatures from the deep

Hairy

Slimy

Shaggy fur

Scales

Tentacles

Forked or spiked tail

Webbed feet

Claws

Fangs

Horns

Dinosaurs and dragons

Lizard-like

Huge teeth

Spikes

Scales

Armoured plates

Dragons also have a fire-breathing tongue, wings like a bat and a long spiked tail

Cyclops

Gigantic

Large single eye

Two left feet

Mummy

Bandaged all over

Main body section can be made in solid, stiffly bandaged format but head and limbs, or at least the legs, should be separate so actor is mobile

Cobwebs and scarab beetles suggest recent emergence from the tomb.

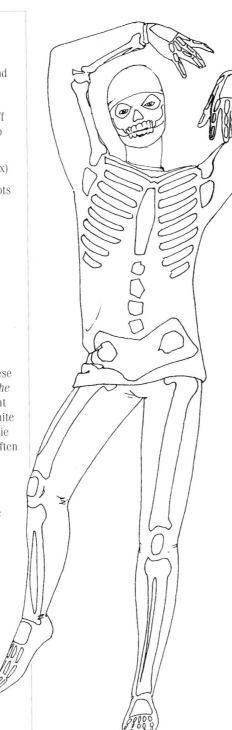

Frankenstein

Black ill-fitting clothes

High square-topped forehead

Heavy eyebrows

Bolts through neck (caps off electric light bulbs stuck to rubber washers)

Scars (staples in Derma Wax)

Long legs so use built-up boots

Big shoulders–pad with foam blocks

Vampire

Scalloped bat wings

Black clothing

Fangs

Arched brow line

Count Dracula

Count Dracula disguises these vampire features *some of the time* and appears in elegant Victorian evening wear, a white satin waistcoat and a bow tie under a swirling long cape–often black with a red lining

Alien

Anything goes–including:

Antennae

Two heads

Pointed elfin ears

Strange skin colour

Distorted humanoid features

Metallic skin texture

Scales

An ET corrugated neck

Skeleton and skull details

Main bone structure: Can be painted on to black body suit, in luminous paint or to show up in an ultra-violet light effect

Skull needs black eye sockets and leering teeth

Death

Basically an ominous figure, portending death to those unfortunates who see him

Skull head–or faceless

Long deeply-hooded black cloak

Pointing skeletal hand

Ghost

White or transparent–sheets or folds of muslin or soft net

A mask made of semi-transparent plastic, cut from a container, is effective

Might be manacled or have a ball and chain–card sprayed silver or cardboard covered with metallic foil (can be painted with black poster paint and glue and then rubbed with a damp cloth to look like duller older metal)

The ghost might be headless –or faceless

Werewolf

Shaggy hairy body

Wolf or dog like

Lots of facial hair, especially low down the forehead or sprouting from brow bone

Canine muzzle

Dog teeth

Mermaid or siren

Conrary to the creatures so far discussed, mermaids and sirens lure men to their death through being beautiful. The interpretation of this character's costume will depend on whether the scene is supposed to be serious, visually pleasing or comic.

Long flowing hair

Ostensibly naked breasts can be suggested by a flesh-coloured body suit or a brief bikini top might be suitably adapted, with shells or strands of mock seaweed.

Seaweed (or strings of general foliage) can be made by cutting zig-zagged ragged strips of green fabric or paper and then stretching out the lengths.

A slim scaly tail can be made from shiny fabric cut into scallops which are sewn on to a plain base fabric, so as to overlap each other.

Iron-on stiffening fabric or self-adhesive fabric bandaging can be cut into scales and stuck onto the base fabric. This can then be sprayed with metallic green–or silver–or icy blue. Random spraying with two colours can be very effective.

Or layers of different coloured net scallops can create a lovely rainbow effect.

Ideally the mermaid should be draped behind a rock with the tip of her tail fin curled up into view. If she has to move this is more difficult as protruding feet ruin the effect. It may be easier if she can be trucked on–or if waves or rocks can be a permanent feature of the costume or, better still, part of the set; she can then enter and exit behind a low level ground row.

Medusa

Medusa, the Gorgon, has a head of snakes instead of hair. In the Original Greek legend these snakes writhe about and turn men to stone.

Snakes can be attached to a buckram wig base, a short-haired wig or a bathing cap.

If your stage structure allows, or if the scenery can be organised to accommodate this, some of the snakes can be played like a marionette and made to wriggle by attaching invisible threads and taking this to a suitable vantage point above or to the side of the monster. Accompanied by loud hissing sounds, this could look very effective.

Abnormal features

Making Medusa's snake wig

Plastic snakes can be bought from joke shops

Snakes can be made from cord, rope or string

Cable can be used. Fabric-covered flex often has good snake-like striping

Heavy-duty 'bungee' elastic is colourfully striped

Or try piped material (see page 31)

Or broad ric-rac braid

Stuffed stockings or toes of tights will make plumper serpents

Making monster heads

Monster heads can be made of papier maché and/or cloth maché (see page 45 for instructions) built up over a balloon or chicken-wire frame.

They can be designed as masks to go over the head or the face, or part of the face. The section on masks (see pages 78-83) describes all sorts of different ways to make masks.

Giants and ogres

Bigger monster heads or giant heads might be designed to sit on the top of the head; this will give extra height and is good for giants, provided the head can be secured well and is not too top heavy.

Really large monster heads can be made to rest on the shoulders or supported on a pole (see page 44). Much greater height is gained if you secure the head on top of a broomstick or a long pole which is held by the actor concealed below under an elongated costume. This works well for relatively short appearances, provided the actor can see well enough to move safely and is comfortable supporting the head in this way. Hoops help to support the costume and retain its shape and also keep the peepholes from flapping about.

Making a monster head from a sack

1 Open out a strong paper sack. Make sure all the folds are properly 'billowed out'.

2 Paste over the sack with several layers of newspaper and paste.

3 Paint the entire head with emulsion paint.

4 When this is dry, extra features like horns, a bulbous nose, eyes, antennae or fangs can be added.

5 When the emulsion is dry, paint in the details.

6 Cut out a mouth, if required, and peep holes for the actor to see through clearly.

7 The head can be attached to a suitable bottom half of costume or worn over trousers or leggings, according to the overall design.

As well as papier maché and sacks, monster heads might also be made of:

Large balls

Balloons–useful if the monster has to be destroyed quickly

Paper bags

Sacks

Cardboard boxes

Calico or other fabric stretched over canes or hoops

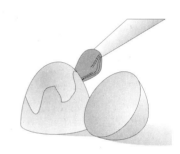

Lightly boiled eggs can be scooped out and painted to make effective staring 'goggly' eyes. Paint them first first with a mix of PVA glue and white paint to make them rigid and then decorate as required.

Grotesque features

Papier maché can be used for ghoulish features but here are few alternative suggestions for materials which, suitably painted or covered in fabric, can be very effective. For further features, such as wings and tails, see the section on animal appendages on pages 74-5.

Mis-shapen bodies

> Bodies can be costructed with:
>
> Hoops
>
> Wire frames
>
> Egg boxes

Blocks of foam can be used to make huge shoulders or to pad out any lumps or bumps.

Rounder shapes like swellings and hunchbacks can be achieved by using kapok or small pieces of foam or chopped-up tights and then stuffing sacks or pads of fabric to be tied with tape onto the actor's body or sewn inside the costume.

> ### Skin and fur
>
> Multicoloured scraps of fabric
>
> Mock leather
>
> Old coats–leather, suede,

Old sweatshirts and leggings or a baggy tracksuit can be given slimy swirls or scales with poster paint or fabric dyes and paint.

Warts and blemishes can be made of rice-crispies or from pieces of odd-shaped macaroni.

Cheesecloth that has been soaked in size, shellac or PVA (white flexible glue) can be squeezed into wrinkles and folds of flesh.

Spaghetti can be softened in hot water and then shaped while pliable. Allow to dry out again in interesting twists and crinkles to use for all sorts of surface effects.

> ### For eyes, try using
>
> Egg shells painted
>
> Ping pong balls
>
> Clay
>
> Fimo
>
> Foam balls
>
> Foil
>
> Marbles
>
> Buttons
>
> Bottle tops
>
> ### Fangs and teeth
>
> Foam
>
> Fimo
>
> Strong cardboard
>
> Pieces of plastic cut from yoghurt containers

Fangs

Fangs will be needed for werewolves and vampires. Plastic fangs from joke shops can be sewn or glued onto a costume or mask. Alternatively, bones from the butcher or a taxidermist can be used but they may need to be boiled and bleached before being pierced into a strip of foam rubber and then glued into place there–ready to be worn in the mouth or sewn onto a costume or a mask.

> ### Noses
>
> Foam
>
> Nose putty from a make-up shop
>
> Clay
>
> Card
>
> Tin foil scrunched and moulded
>
> Fimo
>
> ### Ears
>
> Felt
>
> Foam
>
> Clay
>
> Fimo
>
> Card
>
> Buckram
>
> ### Antennae
>
> Pipe cleaners threaded through egg boxes
>
> Tightly twisted aluminium foil
>
> Wire
>
> Washing-up bottle tops
>
> Toilet roll tubes
>
> Doweling
>
> Bed springs
>
> Plastic piping
>
> Microphones
>
> Toothbrushes
>
> ### Tentacles
>
> Cable
>
> Cord
>
> Sucker pads off children's toys
>
> Felt
>
> Plastic corrugated vent pipe

Hair and beards

String or cord

Wool

Wood shavings

Ric-rac braid

Raffia

Fake fur

Paper

Feather boas

Dry macaroni stuck on a base

Crepe hair from a make-up supplier

Christmas garlands (dark green matte ones are good)

Ask photographers for reels of old film.

Crepe paper slashed and rolled

A few useful tips

See-through gauze can be used as part of a mask or costume to conceal an actor's peepholes.

Rummage through the shelves in joke shops for a fascinating choice of fingers, noses, claws and teeth.

Robots and machines

A robot is a hybrid between a human and a machine. The emphasis can go in either direction—from a veritable walking machine to a humanoid with just a few mechanical 'give-aways'.

To achieve the mechanical effect, whatever the degree, raid junk shops, jumble sales, sheds and garages and put out a plea to everyone involved in the production to provide some of the most useful odds and ends.

Robot features

Old telephones

Electric switches

Light fittings

Egg boxes

Cabling and hose

Dials

Clock faces cut out of magazines

Photographic odds and ends (reels and wheels, film cases and so on)

Nuts and bolts and washers

Bed springs

Knitting needles

Packaging tubing and toilet-roll centres

Plastic bottles and containers

Bottle tops

Bicycle reflectors

Plungers

Silver 'metallic' or heavier gauge shiny white plastic (or paper) plates and cups

Old umbrellas and bicycle spokes

Corrugated card

Metal coat hangers

Ping-pong balls

Polystyrene packing sections

Yo-yos

Coloured lighting gels

Rivets

Flexible metal sheets or metallic card

Foam rubber insulation tubing

It is amazing how effective everyday household items like egg cartons, yoghurt pots and toilet-roll tubes look once they have been sprayed with metallic paint.

Useful tips

An old motor-cycle helmet can be a good base for a robot head. An LED display can be powered by batteries concealed within the costume. Wide corrugated vent hose can go right over a child's limbs and industrial hose might clothe an adult.

Paper maché can be layered inside saucers or bowls (these should first be smeared with petroleum jelly to ease separation) to make small satellite receivers.

Wire or sized string can be wound around tubing to give a turning or cork-screw effect. Wire antennae topped by a ping pong ball and hooks off the top of shower gel bottles can also look effective.

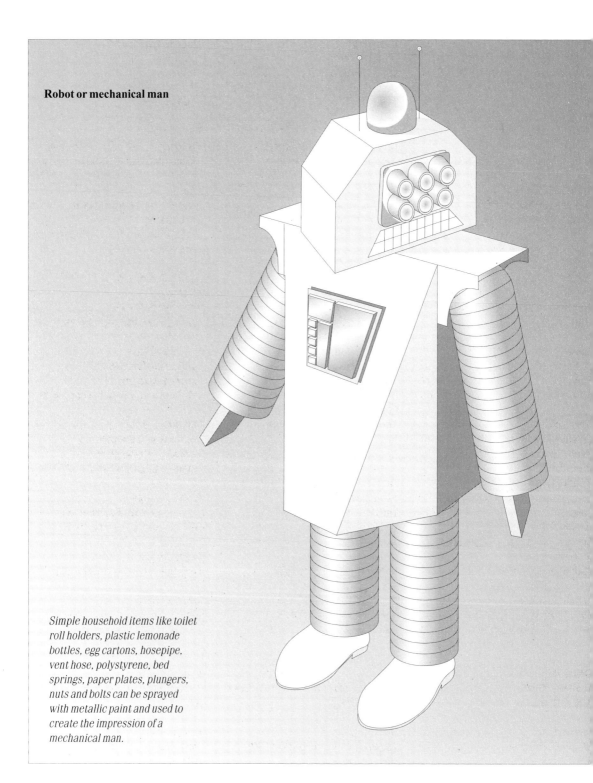

Robot or mechanical man

Simple household items like toilet roll holders, plastic lemonade bottles, egg cartons, hosepipe, vent hose, polystyrene, bed springs, paper plates, plungers, nuts and bolts can be sprayed with metallic paint and used to create the impression of a mechanical man.

Bibliography

Bawden, Juliet
The Hat Book
Charles Letts, London, 1992

Bond, David
The Guinness Guide to Twentieth Century Fashion
Guinness Publishing Limited, Enfield, Middlesex, 1992 1981

Bradfield, Nancy
Costume in Detail 1730-1930
Harrap, London, 1968

Bruun-Rasmussen, Ole and Petersen, Grete
Make-up, Costumes & Masks for the Stage
Sterling Publishing Co. Inc., USA, 1981

Cassin-Scott, John
Costumes and Settings for Historical Plays, Volume 2, The Medieval Period
B T Batsford Limited, London, 1979

Cassin-Scott, John
Costumes and Settings for Historical Plays, Volume 3 , The Elizabethan and Restoration Period
B T Batsford Limited, London

Cassin-Scott, John
Illustrated Encyclopaedia of Costumes and Fashion from 1066 to the present
Studio Vista , London, 1994

Couldridge, Alan
The Hat Book
B.T. Batsford, London, 1980

Evans, Cheryl and Borton, Paula (Editor's.)
The Usborne Book of Dressing Up
Usborne Publishing Limited, London, 1993

Govier, Jacquie
Create Your Own Stage Props
A & C Black, London, 1984

Greenhove, Jean
Party Costumes for Kids
David and Charles, Newton Abbot, Devon, 1988

Hoggett, Chris
Stage Crafts
A & C Black, London, 1980

Holkeboer, Katherine Strand
Patterns for Theatrical Costumes
Prentice-Hall Inc., Englewood Cliffs, New Jersey, USA, 1984

Ingham, Rosemary and Covey, Elizabeth
The Costumer's Handbook
Prentice-Hall Inc., Englewood Cliffs, New Jersey, USA, 1980

Jackson, Sheila
Costumes for the Stage
The Herbert Press, London, 1978

Lewis, June R
From Fleece to Fabric
Robert Hale, London, 1983

Lipson, Michelle
The Fantastic Costume Book
Sterling/Lark, New York, 1992

Mander, Raymond and Mitchenson, Joe
Pantomime: a story in pictures
Peter Davies Limited, London, 1973

Peacock, John
The Chronicle of Western Costume
Thames and Hudson, 1991

Racinet, Albert
The Historical Encyclopedia of Costumes
Studio Editions Limited, London, 1992

Rowland-Warne, L
Costume: Eyewitness Guides
Dorling Kindersley, London 1992

Sichel, Marion
1950 to the Present Day, Costume Reference 10
B T Batsford Limited, London, 1979

Tompkins, Julia
More Stage Costumes (and how to make them)
Pitman Publishing 1975

Young, Douglas
Create Your Own Stage Faces
Bell and Hyman, London 1985

Vogue Sewing
Harper and Row, New York, 1982

Wright, Lyndie
Masks (Creative Crafts series)
Franklin Watts, London, 1989

Other stage books available from A & C Black

Davies, Gill
Staging a Pantomine
A & C Black, 1995

Motley
Designing and Making Stage Costumes
Herbert Press

Nunn, Joan
Fashion in Costume 1200-1980
Herbert Press

Reid, Francis
The Staging Handbook
A & C Black

Reid, Francis
Designing for the Theatre
A & C Black

Index